Prais

From My Hands and Heart

*"**From My Hands and Heart** is an excellent guide to helping you understand the healing power of craniosacral therapy (CST). From Kate's description of her clients' experiences you will see how CST can play a pivotal role in promoting health and balance in your life. In addition you will discover practical ways to integrate your CST experience into your everyday life."*

— Suzanne Scurlock-Durana, founder of Healing from the Core and author of *Full Body Presence: Learning to Listen to Your Body's Wisdom*

"Kate eloquently weaves the stories of her clients' treatments into her explanations. This provides a wonderful illustration and is appropriate, as the premise of CST is to listen to the inner wisdom of clients and their individual stories, trusting that their bodies know what they need. Her passion and knowledge in addition to her 'walking her talk' by getting treated herself is an excellent expression of Dr. Upledger's work. Kate Mackinnon sets a beautiful example of an ideal craniosacral therapist."

— Carol McLellan, CST-D, Upledger Institute International

"Kate's book on craniosacral therapy is unique. Books on CST tend to fall into one of three categories: medical textbooks written for professional instruction, compendiums of case reports describing the results of individual treatments, and memoirs detailing one person's healing journey and their experience of CST. Kate's book is something special in that it manages to bridge all three categories. Her book eloquently describes her personal journey and growth as a therapist. She includes enough technical information on CST so the interested reader can understand the work and many descriptions of treatments she has done on her clients, as well as detailing how CST has helped her on her own road to healing. She describes her own process with passion and humility. I highly recommend her book to any reader interested in alternative medicine or CST."

— Tim Hutton, Ph.D., CST-D

From My Hands and Heart

Hay House Titles of Related Interest

YOU CAN HEAL YOUR LIFE, the movie, starring Louise L. Hay & Friends
(available as a 1-DVD program and an expanded 2-DVD set)
Watch the trailer at: **www.LouiseHayMovie.com**

THE SHIFT, the movie,
starring Dr. Wayne W. Dyer
(available as a 1-DVD program and an expanded 2-DVD set)
Watch the trailer at: **www.DyerMovie.com**

♡

ALL IS WELL: Heal Your Body with Medicine, Affirmations, and Intuition, by Louise L. Hay and Mona Lisa Schulz, M.D., Ph.D.

ARCHETYPES: Who Are You?, by Caroline Myss

THE ART OF EXTREME SELF-CARE: Transform Your Life One Month at a Time, by Cheryl Richardson

THE BIOLOGY OF BELIEF: Unleashing the Power of Consciousness, Matter & Miracles, by Bruce H. Lipton, Ph.D.

SECRETS OF MEDITATION: A Practical Guide to Inner Peace and Personal Transformation, by davidji

WISHES FULFILLED: Mastering the Art of Manifesting, by Dr. Wayne W. Dyer

All of the above are available at your local bookstore,
or may be ordered by visiting:

Hay House USA: **www.hayhouse.com**®
Hay House Australia: **www.hayhouse.com.au**
Hay House UK: **www.hayhouse.co.uk**
Hay House South Africa: **www.hayhouse.co.za**
Hay House India: **www.hayhouse.co.in**

From My
Hands and Heart

Kate Mackinnon

HAY HOUSE, INC.
Carlsbad, California • New York City
London • Sydney • Johannesburg
Vancouver • Hong Kong • New Delhi

Copyright © 2013 by Kate Mackinnon

Published and distributed in the United States by: Hay House, Inc.: www.hayhouse.com® • ***Published and distributed in Australia by:*** Hay House Australia Pty. Ltd.: www.hayhouse.com.au • ***Published and distributed in the United Kingdom by:*** Hay House UK, Ltd.: www.hayhouse.co.uk • ***Published and distributed in the Republic of South Africa by:*** Hay House SA (Pty), Ltd.: www.hayhouse.co.za • ***Distributed in Canada by:*** Raincoast: www.raincoast.com • ***Published in India by:*** Hay House Publishers India: www.hayhouse.co.in

Project editor: Nicolette Salamanca
Cover design: Cynthia Morris • *Interior design:* Pamela Homan

All rights reserved. No part of this book may be reproduced by any mechanical, photographic, or electronic process, or in the form of a phonographic recording; nor may it be stored in a retrieval system, transmitted, or otherwise be copied for public or private use—other than for "fair use" as brief quotations embodied in articles and reviews—without prior written permission of the publisher.

The author of this book does not dispense medical advice or prescribe the use of any technique as a form of treatment for physical, emotional, or medical problems without the advice of a physician, either directly or indirectly. The intent of the author is only to offer information of a general nature to help you in your quest for emotional and spiritual well-being. In the event you use any of the information in this book for yourself, which is your constitutional right, the author and the publisher assume no responsibility for your actions.

Library of Congress Cataloging-in-Publication Data

Mackinnon, Kate
From my hands and heart : achieving health and balance with craniosacral therapy / Kate Mackinnon.
pages cm

ISBN 978-1-4019-4077-5 (pbk.)
1. Craniosacral therapy. I. Title.
RZ399.C73M33 2013
615.8'22--dc23

2012048648

ISBN: 978-1-4019-4077-5
Digital ISBN: 978-1-4019-4078-2

16 15 14 13 4 3 2 1
1st edition, May 2013

Printed in the United States of America

To Claire and Haimish—the light
and joy in my life

and

In memory of Dr. John Upledger
(1932–2012)

CONTENTS

This poem by Nancy Levin was inspired by her experience of craniosacral therapy, and it is reprinted with grateful permission.

whole

while her hands navigate
the map my body makes,
it's the radiating rhythm
of vibration and stillness
that now allows me
to receive what it hides
and translate all it has to tell.

this journey to knowing,
deep in my essence,
that i am loved.
no matter what i do or don't do,
even if i don't do anything i will be loved.

but to believe, i needed courage.
i found it in my body.

my body,
a treasure chest,
its cellular secrets under lock and key
until the moment they were ready to be freed.

in the body
love first develops as hunger.
these walls have cellular memory.
there is a haunting here.

tight fitting skin,
barely wrapping bones
in dehydrated desert conditions
are infused with vitality
fleshed out and expanded
nourished and recalibrated
buoyant.

sensation returning and there,
my breath still held,
i felt full for the first time.

my power is very confusing.
and although my legs just want to run
i can feel my feet begin to find their roots,
sourcing safety for my strength.

i found my grounding
and what feeds me
in asking for help
from an intuitive hand.

my body,
once a fortress,
now begs for entry
and re-entry.

the thaw begins like this,
after being frozen in place
for so long,
waves of flame and prayer
release me,
finally locating the passage
from my heart,
revealing the way to healing.

and so in the softening,
i learn that love
presents in many forms:
in flames on candles carried
in kisses and wishes of peace
in snow surrounding a mountain waterfall.

my body melts
outside its lines.

my thoughts,
my own
for the first time.

and as pieces of me
return or arrive,
desire alone senses
the rise and fall
of what's alive
inside.

and now,
stripped of all
i once defined
myself by,
it takes only a moment
to notice
i have always been
whole.

FOREWORD

A few years back I knew very little about the subject of craniosacral therapy (CST). On a couple of occasions I had been approached by people who called themselves CST practitioners and offered a session. However, the truth is I felt nothing and was unable to notice any appreciable improvements of any kind. Basically I'd experience a relaxing hour, express my appreciation, and that would be the end of the story. While I did not discount the potential healing potentialities of CST, I was somewhat skeptical of this whole idea of moving invisible energy around by feeling rhythms and extending a gentle touch. As the Broadway song from *A Chorus Line* says, I tried it and I felt nothing.

That is until I began a series of surprising and extraordinary sessions of CST with the author of this book, Kate Mackinnon. I had my very first session with Kate back in February 2010, shortly after I had received the diagnosis of chronic lymphocytic leukemia. I was at a very low energy level at the time and still somewhat in shock at this new status in my life. I was blessed to have this exceptional healer give me two CST sessions daily for several days.

From the very first moment of my very first session with Kate, I felt a source of energy moving through my entire body as I lay there on the massage table. That session was a transformative experience for me; when it was complete, I knew that something stupendous had just taken place. Something I couldn't define was happening in my head and traveling down through my spine. I felt reenergized, lighter, and in a state of gratitude to God for having sent this amazing woman to me at that troubling time in my life.

Kate performed two sessions a day with me for four days. On two occasions she actually carried out her CST work on me while I floated in the ocean with her. I went from being a skeptic to a firm believer in this practice as a means to providing healing energy in lieu of the harsher and riskier modalities offered in the allopathic medical model.

I am now in my seventh decade, and after being a very active athlete for my entire adult life—running many competitive marathons, playing tournament-level tennis daily for over three decades, and practicing yoga and long-distance swimming—my body has reacted to this physical fitness regimen with a long list of pains and challenging ailments. I have found that Kate Mackinnon's gentle-touch CST therapy has been an absolute miracle for me in sending away any annoying discomfort.

I call Kate my miracle worker; in fact I have been so impressed and positively impacted by the skill of this woman that I have asked her to work with several members of my family and introduced her to many of my friends and colleagues as well. Without exception, every single person who participated in a CST session with Kate—even those who are most dubious about energy medicine and anything that is a not a sound, scientifically proven medical treatment—had the same reaction as I did.

In the introduction to my recently published book *Wishes Fulfilled,* I included a summary of a CST session that Kate did with a young woman, Nicollette, who suffered from a severe case of Bell's palsy. The elimination of the facial paralysis within a very short time was attributable, in part, to the work Kate did with her.

On a tour of Assisi, Lourdes, and Medjugorje in 2011 called "Experiencing the Miraculous," Kate offered CST sessions to scores of spiritual seekers who went on this journey with me. Without exception the reports that came back were all in the "she is amazing, I feel better than I have in years" category. The same reports always come back whenever I ask Kate to offer a CST session. It is like having a massage for my soul. Indeed, she has taken the practice of CST to an entirely new level of healing.

♡

I have been so impressed by the opportunities that CST offers, not only for healing, but for creating a sense of well-being and inner peace when rendered by an accomplished practitioner, that I asked Kate to write her own book on how to achieve a sense of balance and renewed health through craniosacral therapy. She brings her many years of research and practice to this book that you are about to read.

I am so very pleased to write a few words of introduction to this remarkable book. It is truly a treasure filled with practical tips on how to alleviate tension and stress that have long resided in the body. This is not a technical manual for those who wish to learn how to become a craniosacral therapist; rather, it is written for the layperson who desires to feel better, who wishes to alleviate any nagging discomforts and utilize a healing modality that does not involve prescription drugs or even more radical approaches such as surgery.

I have long believed that there is a spiritual solution to every problem. Having had over 50 sessions with Kate over the past years and having observed her help so many of my friends, colleagues, and family members without the use of any drugs or physical manipulations, I feel the presence of a spirit at work with her in a very big way. This is a subtle and intuitive approach to healing, and Kate has put her own intuition into the writing of this book as well.

After years of study and practice Kate has come to trust in her own abilities to feel through her hands and her heart, and she has skillfully put her subtle healing awareness into the pages of this book. I enthusiastically endorse the work of this highly skilled, intuitive, spiritually based healer, whom I am proud to call my friend and colleague.

I encourage you to pay close attention to what this phenomenal teacher has to offer you concerning craniosacral therapy as an alternative to the far more extreme options that are generally offered through the medical model. I take every opportunity I can to have a CST session with Kate. I treat it like an energy tune-up for my body and my spirit as well. Read this book carefully, with a mind that is open to everything and attached to nothing. It offers you a way to greater health and well-being using a therapeutic method that you may never have considered before.

Craniosacral therapy has become part of my way of life since the day that Kate came to me with her skilled hands, her graceful heart, and her intention to be an instrument of healing for me. Ralph Waldo Emerson once observed that "God enters by a private door into every individual." To me Kate has been God's able and noble assistant. She opened a new door that has brought me to never-before-imagined levels of joy, healing, and wellness. May you experience the same as you begin your own journey with my personal craniosacral therapist, Kate Mackinnon. You are in good hands.

— Dr. Wayne W. Dyer

INTRODUCTION

Since my very first days working as a physical therapist, I've seen how patients' emotional and spiritual well-being deeply connect to their physical well-being. I met scores of patients just before their surgeries, and those who had the smoothest recoveries were the ones who saw their surgery as a means to help them with their next adventures in life. Their positive perceptions of the procedure influenced the outcomes. In contrast, some patients who were admitted into the hospital stated flatly that they had come in to die. No matter what medications, surgery, or therapies they were offered, nothing could be done to alter their chosen path.

With my training in the traditional paradigm of Western medicine, it seemed heretical at first to consider that patients' feelings and perceptions could dictate therapeutic outcomes. However, as I saw time and again, our emotional states do affect how we get sick and how well we heal. When we feel stressed, for example, our nervous systems activate the fight-or-flight response. Many of us are living in a constant state of high alert for one reason or another, which keeps our nervous systems ramped up and prevents us from healing well.

Although my physical therapy teachers insisted that we were implementing a holistic approach, the work felt rote and disjointed, not "whole" at all. We were taught to break things down mechanistically and focus on physical symptoms (for example, "decreased range of motion," "chest pain," or "shortness of breath"), combine this with the right test results, and sum it all up with a final prognosis and treatment plan. We figured that if we got the assessment right, the treatment would work. Meanwhile, our patients' emotional states—and therefore the states of their nervous systems—were not assessed with the same level of rigor.

When I took my first class in craniosacral therapy (CST), I finally began to understand how to use a truly holistic approach to support people to heal. CST could treat my clients' physical symptoms, while also relieving the underlying stresses that were hidden in the body. As I worked with my clients, their long-standing illnesses improved; injuries healed; and chronic pain and tension in the jaw, lower back, and neck disappeared, and didn't return. Traditional medical treatments would've involved painkillers, stretching exercises, or perhaps surgical interventions! Although this is effective in alleviating pain in the short term, it does not address the true source of discomfort in order to prevent it from manifesting in another part of the body. On my treatment table, with CST, I can get to the source of a person's symptoms.

A craniosacral therapist uses gentle touch to map the body's responses to stress and injury—sometimes from a recent accident or illness, and sometimes long-ago trauma—and then supports the body in releasing them. This alleviates pain and discomfort, and promotes healing. CST is a partnership between therapist and patient that reads messages the body is sending through where it holds tension and stress. Once we pay attention to what our bodies know, we have a much better chance of becoming whole again.

♡

I'm frequently asked, "How did you end up learning CST?" I first trained as a physiotherapist (physical therapist) in Scotland in the late '80s. I subsequently worked in hospitals in Oxford and London, spending time in several different areas of medicine before deciding to specialize in pediatrics, and eventually heading a team of community pediatric physical therapists.

I heard of CST for the first time while working with a child with cerebral palsy. When her family told me about it, I was very skeptical. Looking back, I see that I was coming from a place of ignorance—I felt threatened due to a misplaced sense of ownership over my patients' outcomes. My outdated idea of the therapist/

patient relationship was one in which only I knew what was best, and I alone should control the direction of therapy. I thought that this child's family looking to augment her care implied that I was ineffective. I now see that this kind of relationship does a disservice to my patients, and I actively encourage them to research other healing modalities.

CST captured my attention again when my friend Paola received it before seeing her dentist for a complex issue. She experienced amazing relief and insight, realizing that unfelt grief over her mother's death was depleting the energy she needed to heal her problem. After just one CST session, she was able to have a much less invasive dental procedure than had originally been predicted.

After hearing about Paola's results, I decided to go to a CST demonstration at a pediatric physical therapy conference. Unlike many other therapies, an observer often doesn't see much happening, so CST can be very boring to watch. However, for those receiving or performing it, there is a lot of activity that can be felt in the body. I came away not much clearer on what the therapy was, exactly, but I was intrigued by the results people were getting. It wasn't until I moved to the San Francisco Bay Area, and began jumping through the many hoops necessary to get my California physical therapy license, that I took my first CST class with the Upledger Institute. After that, I was completely hooked.

I want to share my journey with you in this book so that you too can glimpse the secrets your body is holding and learn how to release the healthy you. You may have heard the term *craniosacral therapy* but don't know what it's all about. Or maybe you're looking for hope, new options, and solutions to your health problems. You may even be receiving CST now, and still not fully understand how it works.

My aim is to explain the science behind this effective therapy in a way that will be understandable to people with no medical background. You'll also read stories about people who have used CST to support their recovery from a wide variety of health challenges. These case studies will give you a better understanding of not just the theory behind CST, but the practice as well.

Many of my clients have said that they don't know how to describe some of the sensations they've felt during sessions, and have great difficulty telling their friends about it. This is one of the challenges in writing or speaking about CST; since there's an energetic aspect to the therapy as well as a physical one, it can be hard to put the experience into words. In this book, I attempt to give you a concrete framework to understand this work.

Another challenge in writing a book on CST is choosing what information to include, as the field has a long history and a wide scope of practice and application that is always evolving. My training is with the Upledger Institute, which was founded by Dr. John Upledger, the original developer of craniosacral therapy. The Upledger Institute conducts research in the CST field and provides a rigorous curriculum to train practitioners. There are also other schools of thought and training in the craniosacral field that produce talented practitioners. And while there's much discussion about the merits of different theories, at the end of the day I suspect we access the same places in the body and spirit; it's just the theoretical framework that's described in different ways.

If you wish to achieve a more solid grounding in CST, there are many excellent books of a more technical nature concerning Upledger theory and practice that are written for the therapist. However, I felt the existing literature was missing a book that helps laypersons understand the work, inspires them to receive CST, and gives them tools to enhance their experience.

I recommend that you read this book from front to back. The first chapter gives an overview of the therapy and explains how CST is rooted in a deep understanding of the physical functioning of the body as well as the energetic part of ourselves. The second chapter takes a brief look at the history of CST, then describes the training required of a craniosacral therapist, explaining techniques and theories as they're presented in the curriculum. Chapter Three discusses what to expect when you receive a typical CST session, and notes the kinds of changes you may experience as a result of the therapy. In Chapter Four we'll explore one of the foundational concepts of Upledger CST, the "inner wisdom." You'll read examples of how, with the right support, the body knows how to heal itself, and learn how to support your own healing process. Then in Chapter Five you'll read several case studies to highlight some of the many conditions CST has helped resolve.

The last three chapters of the book present ways to become actively involved in your own care and maximize the benefits you can get from CST. Chapter Six discusses how to find the right practitioner and how your CST might fit in with other modalities you are engaged in. Chapter Seven gives you concrete examples of how to maintain your results to get the most out of your CST sessions, both while you're on the table and then at home. Finally, in Chapter Eight I explain simple, hands-on techniques you can do for yourself, your friends, and your family. There is also a Glossary at the end of this book to help you keep track of the vocabulary used in CST, and a Resources section with information on various websites, books, and practitioners that will support you in learning more.

I trust that *From My Hands and Heart* will serve you well, and you'll come to know and love craniosacral therapy as much as I do.

Chapter One

Defining Craniosacral Therapy

I can still clearly recall my first experience of craniosacral therapy. As my therapist began to work, I felt that CST was different from anything I had experienced before: her hands went exactly where I wanted them to go without my saying a word. Her touch didn't probe or hurt at all.

During the session, it became clear that I had not yet fully grieved the miscarriage I had suffered a few weeks earlier. Since my tears had stopped and I was living life normally again, I thought I had moved on. But I learned in that first hour of CST that my body and my heart had not. Physically, I began to feel more open and relaxed through my pelvis. During and after that session, I found myself delving deeper into my grief and shedding fresh tears that helped me heal. It was fascinating to me that it felt safe and natural to be so open in front of my therapist. At the time, I was not used to showing my emotions, and my habit was to stuff all those uncomfortable feelings and sensations away. And yet, despite feeling such deep sadness, I felt very peaceful and relaxed after my session, and that peace stayed with me. I knew without a doubt that I should continue receiving this work.

With just one session, CST had me fully engaged. I wanted to know as much as possible about it, and I started on a journey that has given me my life's work. Many of my clients today show the same curiosity I did: they want to know just what this therapy is about, how it works, why they feel what they do in session, and why my hands go where they need them most. Clients will say they don't know how to explain what they are feeling on the table, yet they know it is important and real. I repeatedly hear, "I know what it feels like for me, but I don't know how to explain it to my friends."

It's clear to me that the best way to understand CST is to receive the work and have it be a felt sense in your body. However, this answers the question only for yourself! By nature, CST is very individualized. A session is tailored to your needs on each day and in each moment, so there are myriad variations you might experience. Techniques vary from session to session, and the insights and sensations experienced will be so very personal. CST experiences are also influenced by the therapists themselves, based on their level of experience, the amount of work they personally receive, the fit between therapist and client, and their other complementary skills. However, there are basic tenets of the work that will help you understand what's happening for you on the table.

In this chapter, I'll provide you with a basic framework of what CST is and explain how it works with both the physical and energetic components of ourselves. Later I'll present a case study to show you how CST helped someone not only deal with chronic pain, but also release long-standing patterns of strain in his body to change many other aspects of his life.

The Power of Safe and Gentle Touch

The most succinct and complete definition of CST I have come across is "the healing power of a gentle touch." This is the phrase used on the front of the Upledger Institute pamphlet for CST, and it's true, albeit a little short on details! When asked, many therapists resort to just describing the process of the therapy. But that's seldom satisfying to people, because it doesn't address how the therapy can help them or what they can expect to experience in a session. And of course, without knowing why someone's asking, it's tempting to just catalog all the kinds of conditions CST can help, and that's not a definition at all.

Craniosacral therapy is a highly effective light-touch therapy that works with the whole body and the source of pain and dysfunction simultaneously. For the most part, our bodies do an amazing job of finding ways to work around the stresses and strains caused by traumatic life experiences, such as chronic stress, childhood falls, or illnesses. Take, for example, an early childhood fall down some stairs: the body might work around pain and stiffness in the tailbone by tucking it forward slightly, lessening stiffness there temporarily but putting strain up the spine in the long term. When a work-around is no longer effective, or the body has too many of them to comfortably function, we feel pain or discomfort.

With CST we recognize that, given proper support, the body will heal itself, creating a custom solution to any problem that is causing discomfort. Therapists place their hands over the area of the body that is most related to the source of the problem, and supports the body both physically and energetically to make whatever corrections it needs. Therapists' hands are trained to feel and monitor changes in the body's tissues to a very high degree of sensitivity. In the process of monitoring what is happening in the client's body, therapists' hands follow change as it occurs rather than making the decision to move a person's body in any given direction. This is a principal difference between CST and most other therapeutic types of bodywork.

♡

Safe, gentle touch—a basic premise of this therapy—has a powerful effect. Touch has been used since ancient times in all cultures for supporting people's healing processes. The need for it is so deeply hardwired into our nervous systems that babies die when they are not touched enough.

Think back to a time when you were under a lot of stress in your life. How often during that time did you withdraw from those around you? In truth, the best support in stressful times would be for you to reach out physically to your friends and loved ones. The act of touching can be a profound and deeply meaningful act. Sometimes all you need during a hard time is a friend to place a hand on your arm and sit with you. And a hug at the right moment can be the perfect support.

We have many nerve endings in our skin that are designed specifically to respond to touch. When we are touched in a way that's supportive and not invasive, we can relax. There's a quality in that kind of touch through which we feel heard. In CST we call this *blending and melding* with the tissue, and it's a cornerstone of the work. An experienced therapist has mastered the highly tuned skill of feeling what's happening within different anatomical structures in the body, such as the bones and soft tissue, with the least amount of intrusion possible. When people first receive this kind of touch they'll often comment on it, saying something like, "I can't tell the difference between your hand and my body. It feels like they are connected."

The Physical Nature of CST

The word *craniosacral* breaks down into *cranio,* which is a prefix that refers to the *cranium,* our skull; and *sacral,* which refers to the *sacrum,* a triangular-shaped bone at the end of our spine that connects with the lumbar vertebrae and the tailbone. These two structures are the outer boundaries of the *craniosacral system.* You can feel the boundaries of your craniosacral system by putting one hand on your head and the other on your sacrum. To find your sacrum, feel down your back along your vertebrae. After you feel the last one at the base of your spine in your lower back, your hand is then resting on your sacrum.

These two bony places, the cranium and sacrum, provide the hard outer protection for the brain and spinal cord, which make up the *central nervous system*. These structures are further supported by membranes that line the bones, and the fluid that fills those membranes, which provide cushioning for the brain and spinal cord. The craniosacral system is at the very core of our being; disturbances in this system create disease or disharmony in the body as a whole. Likewise, problems in the body also reflect back to the craniosacral system, putting it under strain.

The fluid in the craniosacral system is called *cerebrospinal fluid*, and it is vital to the practice of CST. It exhibits a gentle rhythmic motion throughout our lives: the *craniosacral rhythm* (CSR). This rhythm is created within the craniosacral system itself through rising and lowering pressure, and it can be felt anywhere on the body. In most adults, it cycles 10 to 12 times a minute. Craniosacral therapists rely on the CSR for information on how to conduct their sessions. They use it to evaluate how well the body is functioning as a whole, and also to identify and pinpoint where specific difficulties are located. It's so important, one of my most respected teachers tells his students, "If you're not paying attention to the rhythm, you're not performing craniosacral therapy."

Although I had a solid training in anatomy and physiology from my physical therapy training, my knowledge was deepened further when I learned the detailed anatomy involved in CST, such as how the bones of the cranium relate to each other and to the structures and fluid that support the brain from within. This level of detail helped me understand the physical makeup of the craniosacral system, and appreciate how important its smooth functioning is for every system in the body.

The Energetic Nature of CST

In order to receive CST, it's not necessary to believe in the energetic component of the work. You can have effective sessions without even mentioning the word *energy*. Changes felt in the body can be described in words that are already familiar. For example, I may ask clients if they can feel heat coming from the area we are working with. That's the release of energy, but it's just as accurate to say that it's a release of heat. This practical and down-to-earth approach helps just about everybody relate to CST, without there being a "something" you have to believe in for the therapy to work for you.

Talking about "energy" and "energy work" can make people uncomfortable. But if you take a moment to think about it, we come into this world as energetic beings. Babies are very responsive to their environment and seem to have an uncanny ability to sense what is going on. Any mother can tell you that when she's feeling a little out of sorts, her baby is also cranky. (In my case, when my twins were born I had *two* cranky babies on my hands!)

This ability of a baby to judge energetic intent was clearly demonstrated to me when I worked on my friend's newborn, who was just 24 hours old. She had been born at home and was sleeping very contentedly. As I held her and gently checked in with her CSR, she opened her eyes and looked directly at me, as if to say, "Do you know what you are doing?" I assume I passed the test, as she soon closed her eyes and I felt the restriction I had noticed release.

People are familiar with touch: we can see it and feel what we see! With energy, however, we can certainly feel it, but we don't see it. And while you may be comfortable touching your friends and loved ones with a hug or a back rub, most people are not so comfortable with the idea of working with energy, even though it's energy that makes the hug feel comforting and the back rub feel supportive. However, energy is not so strange a concept as some people may think. After all, many of us have had the experience of feeling that somebody is looking at us while our back is turned. I think that we use this sixth sense—our energetic awareness—all the time.

We are energetic beings. Anything that has vibratory motion between its atoms has energy. Even the particles that make up the atom are in motion. In Native American mythology, a stone has its own vibration and, therefore, energy. When I first learned this upon moving to America, it seemed like a bizarre concept to me, but now it seems obvious. Each object has its own molecular makeup, with unique opportunities for movement and vibration. When we start to look closely at our environment, we notice that everything has vibration and an innate intelligence.

Energetic exchanges take place even in allopathic medicine when, for example, therapeutic radiation is used to treat cancer or when ultrasound is used to help with pain and inflammation. Touch also involves an exchange of energy, which influences our being in a powerful way. As craniosacral therapists, we are taught how to pay attention to these changes in the energy system of the body. Most times, as a therapist notices a shift in a person's energy, clients can feel a response in their physical body, usually along with a sense of relaxation, a feeling of the body softening and opening.

The Use of CST in Different Settings

Craniosacral therapy can be combined seamlessly with most medical interventions. Practitioners from both Western- and alternative-medicine backgrounds incorporate CST skills into their work. CST is performed by doctors, dentists, physical and occupational therapists, acupuncturists, massage therapists, and many other types of practitioners. More than 100,000 people in over 60 countries have taken at least one class in CST with the Upledger Institute since its founding some 30 years ago. I think one reason so many practitioners use CST is because it works with the physical structure and function of the body, along with actively working with the body's energetic systems. It's the perfect combination of conventional allopathic medicine and energy medicine.

CST does not need to be a replacement for any other form of treatment; it can be combined with most treatments, whether mainstream or alternative, to create a powerful partnership. I work with many clients who have complex medical needs, and I am just one member of their health-care teams. I usually work in my office, but I have, on occasion, worked with my clients while they're in the hospital. Some of these clients need a lot of medical treatments, and I support their team in helping the outcome be more successful. For instance, no matter how skilled a surgeon may be, surgery is still a significant trauma for the body to heal from. There is also a chemical effect on the body from anesthesia, and the invasive nature of being intubated (inserting a breathing tube). Without help, the body can be left in considerable discomfort. Although the surgical site will heal, the way in which the body does repairs can create strain and tension at the incision or beyond, often leading to pain and restricted movement.

CST helps the body find a more efficient way to heal by releasing strain, resulting in reduced pain and increased range of motion. When the body is under tension, it has to do extra work to compensate. This uses up energy and creates strain. Once we no longer have to work so hard around this built-up tension, we have more energy available to us, and this gives a feeling of greater vitality.

I also often work with people who have had repeated dental work. There is an intimate physical relationship between the roof of the mouth and the bones that form the floor of the brain cavity. And sometimes a lot of force is required to complete a dental procedure, creating a torsion or shear in the tissues of the mouth. This leads not only to an imbalance in the jaw, but a disruption in the smooth functioning of the nervous system. Looking at this strictly from a physical-function perspective, CST can help directly with the bones of the face and jaw, ensuring that they are moving freely, and that the nerves have adequate room. This reduces pain significantly, and in some cases can even correct a misaligned bite.

Dental work is also inherently invasive and is often associated with pain. In a CST session, as the tissues let go of tension, clients often remember their dental procedures. This gives their bodies the opportunity to release any emotions that went along with them. As tissues continue to normalize, it's not uncommon for clients to notice a fleeting taste of the medication that was used. When you hear or read about these things, it certainly can sound weird, but when you're receiving therapy, it just feels great!

Injuries that occur when we're under emotional stress are often more complex and take longer to heal. CST helps the body release those traumas. Imagine knowing that when you next need a dental procedure you can go in relaxed, because any discomfort that comes from that procedure can be relieved. CST sessions can be useful both before and after dental work to support successful outcomes.

Babies and children can also benefit greatly from CST. Working with this population requires that you be very skilled at *palpation* and have a deep understanding of how to hold a *neutral* presence. I have found that children with disabilities are very sensitive to a clinician's therapeutic intent. I've worked with children who have been able to feel my hand held from a distance of a full foot behind them. Some then turned around and tapped my hand away because I was not in a neutral enough place while others have taken my hand and placed it exactly where they needed it.

Amazing benefits can result from working with children. You'll find more case studies later in this book, but I'll share one with you here now.

A woman came to me with her four-year-old son, who was having difficulties paying attention in preschool and sitting still in circle time. He had sensory issues starting from birth: he was a very colicky baby and required medication for reflux. After just one session (which we spent softening his respiratory diaphragm, stomach area, and cranial base), his teachers observed that he was having a much easier time at school and asked his mother if she had been trying anything new at home with him. This was great confirmation for her that progress was being made.

The Importance of the Therapist Receiving CST

One thing I've seen time and again: the clearer I am as a practitioner, the more my clients experience possibilities for change. By "clearer" I mean my equilibrium is not as easily disturbed by what a client might be experiencing. For example, let's say a woman comes to see me with neck pain following a car accident in which she was rear-ended by someone on a cell phone, and I've recently had a similar accident. If I am not neutral, I could easily start remembering the feelings from my own accident. I would not be able to maintain a neutral or a relaxed place in my body: my heart rate would increase and my muscles would tense, changing how my hands connect to the person I'm working on. This would be felt by my client on the table, who would then perceive that it wasn't safe to release the tension and emotions in her body.

Being clear is another way of describing my therapeutic presence, which is the way I act and carry myself (my way of being) that tells my clients they are safe. That's why an essential part of being an effective craniosacral therapist is to receive CST, so that as little unresolved tension as possible is present in my body. All the seasoned practitioners I know receive regular CST sessions and maintain other self-care or spiritual practices that help them stay *grounded* and present as they work. Being less affected by whatever a client is dealing with means that my work is more effective and I will not be drained at the end of the day.

CST has supported me through a lot of events, some routine and some not. For example, I had a CST session right before I went to Europe with Dr. Wayne Dyer on the tour that he was hosting, "Experiencing the Miraculous." Wayne had mentioned that he might have me come onstage to talk a little about CST. I was feeling a great deal of anxiety and concern that I was not going to be good enough. The conversation in my head was, *Who do you think you are, talking about CST when there so many better practitioners than you who should be doing this?* I'm sure many of you have experience with similar kinds of conversations playing out in your head.

In my session I was able to drop into a deep state of relaxation and take a more honest look at the question that was running through my mind. I was able to feel the part of me that could see that I was the perfect person to talk about CST, and could ask myself, *Why not take the opportunity?* Because this was a felt sense in my body and not just an intellectual exercise, it had a lot more power.

I have received CST regularly for more than ten years. There is always something that can be helped and supported in my body. Many times I get off the table and wonder how I coped with life before CST! I've benefited from seeing many different CST practitioners, and from each therapist I've received helpful work and gained valuable insights. I know that receiving CST is something that supports my having a full and happy life.

Case Study: The Golfer

The following is a great example of what can be achieved with CST. This client has received no other form of therapy aside from CST since we started having biweekly sessions over a period of 18 months. Although it does work very well with other treatments, this client's experience shows what CST alone can help accomplish. His story gives a real-life example of the material I presented in this chapter, as well as examples of how change is perceived by a client both on the table and then in daily life. I'll briefly explain unfamiliar concepts as they come up, but I also encourage you not to worry about understanding every detail, and to just absorb the story. I'll discuss everything in greater depth as you continue through the book.

♡

One afternoon I received an urgent call from a regular client who was concerned about her husband, Jim, who would be leaving on a 14-hour flight to China in a few days' time. He had acute right knee pain and was unsure whether he would be able to walk once he got off the plane. Jim's job required frequent travel, and on a recent return from an international business trip, he had barely been able to disembark. He had already had two arthroscopic surgeries on each of his knees; the last surgery had been only a month ago, on the left one. He was certain that he would need a third surgery on his right knee and was ready to schedule another MRI. Even more than the constant pain, Jim feared losing his ability to play golf, which was his joy and passion in life.

Until this point Jim had been unwilling to try CST because he didn't understand it, even though his wife had received a lot of benefit from it. Although CST has become more common in the last 30 years, it's still not widely known, and many people, like him, have a healthy skepticism. Other than receiving a couple of massages that hadn't been effective in reducing his pain, Jim had never tried any treatment outside of conventional medicine.

For some people it takes reaching a crisis point to be willing to try something that is outside of their "tried and tested" world. Often they've gotten frustrated by the lack of progress they've had in resolving their pain, and they've exhausted all the options they know of. They feel disempowered, and don't know the next step to take. It took reaching this point of desperation for Jim to give CST a go!

Since Jim was due to fly out on Sunday, I put my treatment table in the car and drove to his home on Saturday morning to see if CST could help him have a more comfortable and manageable trip. Once Jim was comfortably on my table, I placed my hands on several locations, starting at his feet, to feel the craniosacral rhythm throughout his body. One of the things the CSR does is let me know how well a body is functioning in terms of its vitality. If I feel a "drag" in the CSR, I know the client doesn't have the full amount of energy that should be available and that the person will be feeling tired and run-down. I didn't feel a decrease in vitality in Jim's CSR, so I knew his system had plenty of energy.

By feeling Jim's CSR, I could also get a better sense of where the primary cause of his pain was. This may seem counterintuitive, but the source of a problem is not necessarily where the pain is! By tuning in, I assessed that my client's knee pain was stemming at least in part from his sacrum, quite a distance away. I could feel where his body was struggling to work well, especially in both knees and in his lower back, more so on the right than the left. There was very little movement in his sacrum and a decrease in the CSR through his neck and at the base of his skull. Because his head tilted to the left both when he was upright and when he was lying down, I decided to evaluate his *fascia* and noticed a fascial restriction at his right knee and hip that ran through the pelvis and up to the neck.

Fascia is a connective tissue that provides internal support for our bodies, from head to toe and side-to-side, much like a body stocking. You can see fascia very easily on a raw chicken breast; it's the opaque film just under the skin, wrapped around the muscle. Because fascia creates a web to support the whole body, pain in our cheekbone could have its source in the fascia down in the respiratory diaphragm. Imagine an elastic cord that's gotten snagged at one end: the cord would be restricted in how much it could stretch at the point where it got snagged. It could stretch downward from that point on, but in order to be able to lengthen to its full reach again, it must be released from the place it first got caught.

We all have such "fascial snags," and for the most part, we function just fine. We generally have a good amount of flexibility, so we have many ways to work around our snags. But when a body has too many snags (or one or two big ones), then it runs out of options, our movement is restricted, and we feel pain!

After performing this initial evaluation, I had a good picture of Jim's body and an idea of how treatment would proceed. In this case, the origins of my client's knee pain were in his sacrum and right hip, and his neck was involved, as well. He was really surprised that by placing my hands on a few different places on his body I could tell him where his pain originated. The skepticism that he came in with was becoming curiosity.

As I started to treat his sacrum and lower abdomen, not only did I feel a gradual softening in the tissue under my hands, but Jim became aware of just how tight this area had been. It's not unusual that he hadn't noticed the tension he had been holding in that area. Generally, we're not used to really feeling our bodies. Once an acute pain has subsided a bit, we become used to it, and even though there is still discomfort there, we stop paying attention. During a CST session, we become more aware of sensation in our bodies. To that end, Jim told me that he could feel the pain in his right knee intensify as I worked on his sacrum, and there was a tingling sensation running down his legs and out his feet. I became very excited, as I recognized this tingling as a sign of the nervous system letting go of the fight-or-flight response in his body.

When we are stressed or feel we're in danger, our sympathetic nervous system mobilizes a huge amount of energy to confront that danger or get away from it. If our bodies are overwhelmed, we also may faint. This can happen in the blink of an eye, before we're even consciously aware of feeling scared. Once the danger has passed, the parasympathetic nervous system allows us to safely relax and get on with our everyday business. Most likely you have felt this in your own body or seen it in an animal, as it starts to tremble once it knows it's safe. This trembling is a discharging of the energy that got mobilized to cope with danger. Once that's finished discharging, the animal moves on, calm and unperturbed.

The tingling that Jim felt going down his legs was a parasympathetic response; his body no longer had to work at containing and holding in that fight-or-flight energy. Unlike with animals, the process of letting go of the fight-or-flight response often does not come naturally to people. It's as if it gets packaged away somewhere in us, taking a lot of energy and effort to keep it stored. One client described it as having put her difficulties in a box with a locked lid, and she didn't want to look in that box. The problem is that our bodies are taxed by the amount of constant effort that's required to keep that fight-or-flight energy packaged away, and it doesn't allow us to fully relax. As we let go and allow the shaking or trembling to happen and then subside on its own, we have more energy available to us, and we can then find a deeper state of relaxation and rejuvenation from which the body can start to heal itself.

Our ability to heal ourselves is one of the tenets of CST. As Dr. John Upledger stated: "The therapist does not heal or cure. The healing is done by the patient using the help and facilitation of the therapist."

Because of the partnership between therapist and client, sessions are most effective when clients are able to track sensation in their bodies, just as Jim did by reporting the tingling sensation in his legs. Often this is the first time clients have really paid attention to sensations in their bodies, and the therapist can help educate the clients in developing this skill. By being willing to be active participants, clients will gain much more from their sessions. And as they continue with craniosacral therapy, they can become extremely perceptive to even subtle changes.

Results

Jim flew to China the next day, and although his knees were very painful at the end of the flight, he was not immobilized as he had feared. After he returned, he continued with biweekly sessions. After his fourth CST session he was taking two-mile walks daily, his knee pain was much reduced, and he noticed lower back pain only after playing two rounds of golf in the same day! Jim's skepticism disappeared, and he knew that CST was the correct route for taking care of himself.

Over a further 18 months of regular treatments, Jim noticed many positive changes that went well beyond healing his knees. These kinds of life changes often happen when clients deepen their relationships with themselves, which is nearly inevitable with regular therapy. For example, as Jim and I were working through a restriction in the upper part of his rib cage, a memory came back to him of having had pleurisy many years ago. He recalled how scary that had been and how the pain had been so intense, he thought he was having a heart attack.

This would be a frightening experience for anyone, but for Jim it also triggered the memory of his father dying of a heart attack when Jim was nine years old—and interestingly, Jim developed pleurisy when his children were also around nine years old.

As we worked together on his rib cage, the entire area softened and Jim felt more able to take a full, deep breath. He commented that he had always been fearful of having any kind of chest pain, but now that he understood the story behind the fear he could relax more.

This story of pain and synchronicity is a great example of how the energy of life events layers up in the body, gradually demanding attention. For the most part, we experience upsetting events and then continue on with our lives; however, as we continue to ignore uncomfortable emotions and sensations, more layers of life's events build up, and our bodies start to protest. This commonly shows up in the form of pain, lack of energy, and a feeling of anxiety.

I was often drawn to work on the area over Jim's right hip for many of our sessions. Then one day, about a year into our work together, I asked him if he could remember anything about his right hip or leg from childhood. He said he recalled being told that he had been treated for a right hip problem as a baby. He also remembered being treated by a chiropractor because his head was always tilted to the left. These memories had been tucked away for a long time; he did not recall these events during our first session together, and even his wife of 30 years had not known.

After the session he contacted his aunt, who verified that he had been in a hip brace when he was a baby, though that had not stopped him from being a top high-school athlete and running 50 to 60 miles a week as a young adult. Jim's knee pain first started when he was 30 years old, and he progressively limited his activity over time. It's possible that his head tilt was compensation for what was happening at his right hip, which eventually led, decades later, to knee pain.

Our ability to forget significant life events, and to function despite them for quite some time, can be surprising. I once worked with a woman who experienced constant headaches and had been advised to keep increasing her medication until the headaches were helped by it. Even at her maximum dose she felt little relief, and experienced many unpleasant side effects. At her first session I asked her if she had ever had a concussion, and she responded that she hadn't. But as she arrived at her second appointment, she announced, "You know, I just remembered that I was hit on the head by an ax when I was nine, and was knocked out." It seems like someone would never forget something like that, but we do! After three sessions her headaches had been reduced significantly, and she felt like she finally had gained the relief she'd been seeking.

As Jim and I continued to work together, we discovered that a restriction at the first vertebra in his neck also related to his knee pain. He became very adept at tracking sensation in his body, and was intrigued by the fact he might feel strong sensation in one area of his body when I was working over a different area. This deepening awareness helped him to fine-tune his daily activity levels and know when he needed to take a break.

Jim has made many seemingly spontaneous changes in his lifestyle since he began CST. I believe that he had the ability to follow through with these changes because he was not spending so much energy compensating for the stuck areas in his body. He's gone from drinking two or three diet sodas daily to drinking them only occasionally and has lost 30 pounds by changing his eating habits (which also cut his cholesterol levels by half!). He also significantly cut down his alcohol intake; even as he has been dealing with a lot of challenges at work, for the first time in his life he has not used alcohol to deal with the stressful feelings.

The Bottom Line

Jim's seen a lot of improvements in his life since working with me, but what really sold him on CST is the improvement in his golf game. When he plays golf soon after a treatment, his score is three or four shots lower, so he always likes to book one before tournaments! He is delighted that he can now play two rounds of golf pain-free in the same day.

Jim has developed some good self-care strategies, too. He bought the CD that I play during treatments and now has a Pavlovian response to the music! As soon as he hears the first notes, he can feel his nervous system starting to relax. He plays it when traveling and whenever he has trouble getting to sleep. I also helped him develop a maintenance routine of exercises and stretches for his knee and back, while he continues his golf games and daily walks.

Jim now weighs the same as he did when he was in high school, is able to walk and play golf regularly, and has more balance in his life. He's changed his coping mechanisms significantly. He's committed to the lifestyle changes he's made and has become more interested in the process of making these changes rather than only focusing on getting to the end result. He still does not understand how CST works, but because he continues to get the results he wants, he's now more open to looking at other things he doesn't understand, like his wife's spiritual practice.

Both Jim and his wife receive regular CST sessions, and they've noticed that their relationship has improved since they started seeing me. It's given them a shared experience to talk about together and has facilitated a deeper level of connection. Their conversations now are long and wide-ranging, whereas before they were more focused on things that needed to get done. They've also started sharing more activities, such as taking walks and playing golf together.

Again, these kinds of shifts are possible when we no longer have to work so hard at holding restrictions in our bodies and we become more comfortable with feeling different emotions and their accompanying sensations. This is one of the wonders of CST:

what is possible when we have a greater amount of life force available to us. Solutions arise with ease and little analysis. Once we come to a place of balance in our nervous system, we have access to our natural vitality.

I hope you appreciate Jim's case, as it illustrates some of the basic concepts of CST and highlights how CST can help with addressing physical pain and support life shifts through energetic change. Since the integration of academic knowledge with intuitive information is something that keeps me excited about this work, in the next chapter I'll go into greater depth about the "nuts and bolts" of CST.

Chapter Two

Craniosacral Therapy in Depth

In this chapter I present a therapist's view of craniosacral therapy. You'll read about how I learned the work and the mechanics of the physical techniques I use, as well as the expansion of my awareness and the fine-tuning of my sensitivity. Taking you through the process I went through will show you the depth of training that is required to become a competent craniosacral therapist. You'll also gain a more detailed and nuanced understanding of how CST works. By having this background knowledge, you will have a better sense of how this therapy can help you.

At times I present some detailed anatomy, which you don't necessarily need to memorize in order to receive an effective session. You can skim these parts if you like, but I've found that many people enjoy learning more about how their bodies work. To that end, during therapy sessions I often retrieve my model skull so clients can see the structures we've worked on. I may also show pictures from my collection of anatomy books, to give a better sense of a particular structure or system. As we discussed, it's best to be an active recipient in CST, and having a picture in your mind's eye of what your body wants to work on can speed up the process of healing.

A Brief History of Craniosacral Therapy

The roots of craniosacral therapy are in osteopathy, a branch of medicine. In the United States, a doctor of osteopathy (D.O.) practices in the same capacity that a medical doctor (M.D.) does, but has additional training in osteopathic manipulative techniques. In the 1800s A.T. Still, known as the father of osteopathy, created a new perspective of the human body by combining hands-on healing techniques found in cultures around the world with engineering principles. He saw the body as an integrated whole rather than a collection of parts and believed that the body, when given proper support, would heal itself. He is quoted as saying, "The mechanical principles on which osteopathy is based are as old as the universe."

One of Still's star students was Dr. William Sutherland, who became particularly intrigued by the cranium and its influence on the nervous system. He experimented with a helmet fitted with screws to apply pressure on his own cranial bones, and noted various symptoms related to different areas of compression. He determined that cranial bones did, in fact, move, and developed techniques to allow motion to come back to cranial bones that were stuck, thereby normalizing function. Sutherland continued to study the nature of the craniosacral system for the next 50 years, and the subtleties he worked with became a kind of spiritual path for him. He called his work "osteopathy in the cranial field," which developed into what is now commonly known as cranial osteopathy. Students of his founded the Osteopathic Cranial Academy, which continues to teach his work today.

Although craniosacral therapy is inspired by the work of Drs. Still and Sutherland, its practice is very different from what an osteopath or a cranial osteopath offers. As I mentioned previously, CST was founded by Dr. John Upledger, who graduated from osteopathic medical school. However, he didn't become interested in the craniosacral system until 1972, when he was assisting a surgeon who was removing plaque from a patient's *dura mater* (the sheath that surrounds the spinal cord). Dr. Upledger's job was to hold the dura mater still, but he couldn't because it exhibited a unique rhythmic pulsation. This inspired him to study cranial osteopathy and research the craniosacral rhythm, which led to the development of CST, his lifelong passion.

Dr. Upledger joined the biomechanics research department at Michigan State University in 1975 and did much research proving the existence of the craniosacral system. He worked closely with a physicist to measure the changes taking place in his patients as he worked. This process helped him identify and articulate what he was responding to as he worked with his patients. He coined the phrase *craniosacral therapy* and developed a method of training practitioners, creating the curriculum that is taught at the Upledger Institute today.

One of the many innovations credited to Dr. Upledger is his focus on normalizing tension in the membranes attached to the cranial bones. There are vertical and horizontal membranes running though the brain, providing the brain with some structural support. Since these membranes are made of fascia, and connect with the fascia of the body (that body stocking of connective tissue I mentioned in the last chapter), Upledger CST is a whole-body therapy.

♡

I knew as soon as I took my first class with Dr. Upledger (or Dr. John, as he preferred to be called) that he had no qualms about speaking his mind. And with the difficult path he chose as he developed CST, it's clear that he needed that characteristic! For example, during his time at Michigan State, he worked regularly at a school with a high population of children with autism. He found that the children responded well to his therapy, but required ongoing treatment to maintain their results. Therefore, he made the controversial decision to teach the school staff how to do the work. His fellow osteopaths gave him a lot of flak for extending training to people not in the medical field, but Dr. John knew that with competent instruction, laypeople could use the techniques he'd developed safely and effectively.

Few masters of their craft can teach others to do their work well, and I'm grateful that Dr. John was committed to ensuring that competent CST training was available to the most people possible. It was inspiring to watch the master in action as he demonstrated CST, combining his highly attuned intuition with his in-depth knowledge of the anatomy and physiology of the human body.

Dr. John believed that to do CST effectively, practitioners need:

— Thorough knowledge of anatomy and physiology, so therapists can be detailed, precise, and appropriate with their palpation and pressure. (Anatomy and physiology is thoroughly addressed in classes within the Upledger Institute curriculum.)

— An open heart and good therapeutic intent. It is a lifelong process to refine the art of staying in a grounded, neutral, non-judgmental, and open place with our clients.

— The ability to follow their hands. I describe this as my hands "listening" to the tissues. My hands move in response to the tissue movements underneath them. I'm not making a decision to go to any particular place, but instead I work from the premise that my client's body knows how to heal itself, and my role is to follow its direction and provide support.

— To know their limits. As practitioners, it's important to have a sense of our own boundaries and to willingly refer clients to other professionals when appropriate. It is also vital for us to continue to receive our own CST treatments in order to keep our bodies and minds healthy and to keep growing as practitioners.

Feeling the Craniosacral Rhythm

My physical therapy training had been based in medical science, with an emphasis on using studies to prove effectiveness of treatment. I enjoyed it and continue to be excited by new research, but my training had not encouraged me to explore the benefits of incorporating the right, intuitive side of my brain in my work.

When I took my first CST class, I had no difficulty with the detailed anatomy and physiology being presented. However, I was really challenged when it came to letting my guard down and suspending my left, analytical brain so that I could get into a relaxed space to feel the subtleties of the craniosacral system. I knew that I would have to work on developing this area—craniosacral therapists are encouraged to use both the left and right sides of their brains to help clients, embracing all aspects of their brains' skills and functions.

I was delighted when, on the second day, I first felt the movement of the craniosacral rhythm. I spent a lot of time in class getting familiar with it. Initially, my brow was furrowed and my face was tense, but once I felt the rhythm I was in a state of open wonder and relief. Now I get such joy watching people's faces when they first feel the CSR. (You too can learn how to feel this rhythm, and I will take you through the process in detail in the last chapter.)

The craniosacral rhythm can be felt anywhere in the body. It requires a very light, relaxed touch of about five grams of pressure, which is nearly the weight of a nickel. This is very different from the palpation skill that is usually used in manual therapies, where there is deep probing into tissue and joints. Instead of quickly sinking my hands into the tissue to feel what was going on, I had to learn to allow the CSR to come to my hands. In doing so, I could feel a subtle motion of all the skin, tissue, and bones under my hands rolling outward (known as the external rotation, or *flexion,* in CST terminology). This was followed by a slight pause, then a rolling in (known as the internal rotation, or *extension*).

If you're like me, and the analytical side of your brain likes to keep busy, it may help you to form a mental picture of the system that creates this rhythm. We'll start with the structure of the cranium.

The bulk of our cranium is made up of seven bones: the *occiput* at the back of the head, two parietal bones on top, two temporal bones at the sides, the frontal bone at the front, and the *sphenoid* bone behind our eyes with its two wings at our temples. In class, we learned that the adult cranium is not a single fused mass of bones, as the British and American anatomical textbooks taught (and still teach today). The places where the cranial bones connect to one another are called *sutures,* and not only do they allow for microscopic movement to accommodate changes in fluid pressure, they are constantly changing in response to alterations in the internal environment of the body.

A system of fascial membranes lines the cranial bones and also runs vertically and horizontally inside the cranium, separating the brain into four quadrants and providing structure and support. The membranes running vertically are called the falx cerebri and falx cerebelli. The horizontal membrane is the tentorium cerebelli, with its superior and inferior (upper and lower) leaves. This membrane system exits the cranium through a hole below the brain stem called the foramen magnum, forming a protective sheath for the spinal cord and connecting with the rest of the body's extensive fascial network.

The brain and spinal cord are bathed in about 150 milliliters of cerebrospinal fluid, a clear, plasma-like fluid extracted from the blood. Its physical makeup is equivalent to fresh river water, while the makeup of the rest of the fluid in the body is saline, like the ocean. In fact, we have the same proportion of "river water" to "salt water" in our bodies that the earth does: 3 percent river water to 97 percent salt water.

The cerebrospinal fluid is encased by the fascial membrane system I described above, which collectively is called the *meninges*. The dura mater, which is Latin for "tough mother," is the outermost membrane of the system and provides a durable, watertight sheath. Inside the dura mater are two membranes that closely cover the brain and spinal cord, the arachnoid layer and pia mater. Cerebrospinal fluid enables our brain to float in the head and our spinal cord to move freely down our spines, providing a cushioning effect as well as bringing in nutrients and clearing away waste from the nervous system.

The craniosacral system's rhythmic activity is derived from the movement of the cerebrospinal fluid, just as the cardiac pulse derives its movement from the circulation of blood. To explain how this rhythm is created, Dr. John developed the pressurestat model: when pressure in the head reaches an upper threshold, nerves between cranial bones, known as stretch receptors, send a signal to stop cerebrospinal fluid production. This fluid is always draining from the system, so when production stops, the pressure drops. When pressure reaches a lower threshold, receptors signal the need to start producing the fluid again.

It may help to imagine a bathtub with a leaky plug. You want the water to stay at a comfortable depth, but the plug is leaking and a constant trickle of water is going down the drain. Whenever you see the water level drop, you turn on the tap until the water is back to where you want it. This is the basic process that creates the CSR.

♡

There's a lot of information to gain by feeling someone's craniosacral rhythm. As a therapist, I can assess the range, or amplitude, of a person's rhythm by noticing the flexion and extension of the CSR (how far it rolls out and in). By placing both hands symmetrically on the left and right sides of the body at the feet, thighs, pelvis, rib cage, shoulders, and skull, I can get an overall impression of well-being and where any difficulties are in a client's body.

I can also compare symmetry on the left and right sides of the body to help pinpoint difficulties. For instance, if there is half the range of motion of the CSR at the right ankle compared to the left, then I know that there is a problem with the function of the right ankle. I also note the quality of the rhythm overall, as this gives an impression of the person's sense of well-being and energy.

As my palpation skills have deepened, I've become able to feel more subtle information and refine my locating skills. While in my early days I may have noticed a restriction on the left side of the pelvis, I can now hone in on its precise location, for example the left psoas muscle or the head of the left thigh bone. This has allowed me to work more precisely and efficiently.

It is important to keep an open mind and trust my palpation skills when meeting each new client. Clients share some of their history with me before I feel their CSR, and they often have theories about what is wrong. If I do not remain open and neutral, this may lead me to think that I already know where restrictions will be. However, it is important to challenge any assumptions my client or I may have, so I do not miss the true source of the problem. Therapists must set aside a client's history as much as possible during a CST session and pay full attention to what the body is saying—the CSR helps us do that.

The Ten-Step Protocol for the Whole Body

Feeling the craniosacral rhythm is the first of three CST evaluation techniques. Before we go into detail about the other two techniques, fascial glide and arcing, I'd like to discuss the two *ten-step protocols* used at the Upledger Institute to familiarize therapists with the tools and concepts of CST.

Students at the Institute begin by learning a whole-body, ten-step protocol of treatment. They start by using the CSR to assess the body, then gently open up the tissue at the sacrum and pelvis, the respiratory diaphragm at the rib cage, the thoracic inlet at the collarbones, the throat, and the base of the neck. At each of these five places, therapists will put one hand on the front of the body, and the other on the back of the body. (For example, at the pelvis, one hand is under the sacrum and the other hand is placed over the lower abdomen, directly above the sacrum.) Once his or her hands connect, or blend and meld, with the tissue there, the therapist then allows them to follow any movement that is felt, trusting the body's *inner wisdom* to guide what needs to happen to create ease. Blending and melding is a way of touching a person with the least amount of intrusion possible, while the therapist allows, trusts, and accepts the information that comes into his or her hands. The protocol dictates very specific techniques to create space between the first vertebra and the cranium, and a precise order for opening up restrictions between the cranial bones, releasing tension in the mandible (jawbone), and mobilizing the dura mater from the sacrum all the way to the cranium.

The protocol also includes the concept of the *still point.* This is the act of intentionally bringing the CSR to a therapeutic stop. While therapists follow the flexion and extension of the rhythm, they use their hands to very gently create a stop at the end of an extension. This allows an opportunity for the body to self-correct and clear areas that are restricted or not running smoothly. Still points also help create balance in the craniosacral system overall, and give the recipient a feeling of relaxation—clients often release a sigh right before the rhythm spontaneously starts up again. While our bodies naturally go in and out of still points throughout the day, inducing one feels especially nice. It's just another of our innate self-healing mechanisms that we get to enhance with CST.

Beginning craniosacral therapists often follow the ten-step protocol. It is a safe yet effective practice that still has the potential to bring much benefit to recipients. There is minimal risk of harm to clients: for the most part they notice improvement, and in a worst-case scenario they notice nothing at all.

When I first started courses at the Upledger Institute, my classmates and I were advised to practice this protocol at least 70 times before taking the next class in the curriculum. I bought a massage table and asked almost everyone I knew if they would be willing guinea pigs. In fact, at the end, many of my volunteers wanted repeat sessions and reported results like relaxation and less joint pain. One friend, who had been trying to conceive for quite a while with no success, got pregnant.

I found that my commitment to practicing the protocol 70 times paid off, as it helped me understand the logic behind it. I became skilled at feeling the kinds of changes that each step creates in the body. In all of the sessions I carry out now there are still elements of this protocol.

Neutrality

Neutrality is a concept that is central to Upledger CST; it is introduced during the very first class and continuously emphasized throughout. When we touch people, even in everyday situations, we have a natural tendency to either send energy in or take energy out. Sending energy in is most common.

Usually, we're completely unaware of this give-and-take of energy. However, you can more fully understand this concept by thinking of your interactions with friends and family. There are some people who make you feel very energized by being in their company, giving you a lift, while others can make you feel drained.

My natural tendency is to send energy in when I place my hands on people. This most likely comes from my wanting to help them and fix whatever might be wrong. Of course, the trap here is that I want to fix them in the way I think they "should" be fixed! When we mindlessly send energy in, it may not be what is needed; if so, no matter how good our intentions, it is uncomfortable for the person receiving our touch.

Working from a place of neutrality is ideal because only then can we be sure we're acting in the best interests of our clients, open to whatever the person on the table needs in the present moment. In order to hold this place of neutrality, we must hold as little judgment as possible about the other person and ourselves—which is easier said than done! Still, striving for neutrality creates a discipline of catching when we start forming ideas about what "should" be happening or predicting the outcome. The more awareness we can bring to monitoring our own biases, the easier it is to find a neutral place.

When it comes to CST, as in life, none of us likes to be told what to do; and we are soon able to detect any agenda someone may have planned for us! Clients make the most progress when the body's own wisdom is being followed, not the ideas of their therapist. The bottom line is that when human beings are touched in a neutral way, we feel great, like somebody is *really* paying attention to us.

Working with the subtleties involved in finding a neutral place is a continuous and fascinating process. In the last chapter of this book, I present an easy exercise that will show you what your natural tendency is and how to work toward being more neutral.

Mouth Work: The Second Ten-Step Protocol

I was excited to learn more and deepen my knowledge, and the second class in the Upledger curriculum did not disappoint. Here I learned another ten-step protocol that adds on to the first, working predominantly on the structures in and around the mouth. Restrictions in this area can easily have an impact on the craniosacral system, as it is located so close to the brain.

It was fascinating to learn about all the bones and muscles of the face, especially since I had not learned it in detail during my physical therapy training in Scotland. During my first year of training, we'd worked in groups of six as we dissected cadavers in the anatomy department of the University of Edinburgh. Because the dental students had the head, we physical therapy students missed out completely on working firsthand with the structures of the head and face.

In this second ten-step protocol, we began by learning how to open up the throat area more by working with the *hyoid* bone. This horseshoe-shaped bone is held in place by muscles that pull downward to the chest, back to the bones of the cranium and neck, and upward toward the floor of the mouth. This area is a vulnerable, sensitive part of the body and readily holds tension, so it helps to work this easily unbalanced bone with gentle precision.

We then learned a technique to release the muscles that form the floor of the mouth and the tongue. We worked inside the mouth (with gloved hands, of course) to release the cheekbones (zygomata), the roof of the mouth (maxilla), and smaller bones a bit deeper in the hard palate called the vomer and palatines. These structures are very delicate, and any disruption can have a profound effect on a client's sense of well-being—as anybody who has had extensive dental work already knows!

With many of these techniques, the therapist must have clear knowledge of the anatomical structure of an area and make precise, appropriate contact to allow a release of tension. Often, the pressure used needs to be lighter than the standard five grams mentioned earlier.

I have personally experienced amazing changes after receiving this protocol. Jaw pain that I had for years completely disappeared, and today the roof of my mouth feels very different than it once did. The first time I received this work, the roof of my mouth felt so open and spacious that I could see in my mind's eye the vaulted ceilings and high arches of a large cathedral. Now that I receive mouth work regularly, I am able to quickly notice whenever my jaw has tension and easily let it go. By being more sensitive to changes, I can catch a small problem quite early and therefore prevent it from becoming a big problem down the road.

Consider receiving CST sessions if you are dealing with issues in your mouth such as clenching, temporomandibular joint disorder (TMD), orthodontic braces, or any kind of complex dental work. An amazing number of my clients grind or clench their teeth at night, and most of them have jaw pain. The jaw is directly linked to the fight-or-flight response in our bodies and is one of the most common areas in which we hold stress. Anatomically, it's a complex joint, and many different components can be the cause of pain and discomfort in this region. CST is an excellent approach to treating jaw pain, as it treats imbalances in a variety of areas. CST can help long-standing TMD, and is often combined with biofeedback techniques and the work of other health-care practitioners (such as dentists and physical therapists).

Along with physical conditions, CST mouth work can also help with other aspects of one's life. For example, in the Upledger teachings, the structures of the upper chest, throat, and mouth are known as the *avenue of expression*, and releasing these structures gives us more than just physical freedom.

Once I learned techniques to release these areas, I felt that I better understood common phrases such as "being tongue-tied," "biting my tongue," "swallowing my words," and "keeping my mouth shut." Indeed, my teacher warned us that by the end of the class we might not be as restrained as we usually were in what we say! After all, when any of us releases the avenue of expression, we are more likely to speak our truth.

Fascia and Fascial Glide

We discussed fascia briefly in the first chapter, during Joe's case study. Understanding the important role it plays in the body helps reinforce the fact that the location of a symptom may not be the origin of the problem.

Fascia is a type of soft tissue that supports every structure in our bodies. It creates a single weblike system, for the most part running lengthways, from head to toe; and, as you read earlier in this chapter, even the brain is supported by fascial structures. At vital stress points in the body, tough bands of fascia run horizontally. The primary horizontal bands are at the pelvis, the respiratory diaphragm, the collarbones, the hyoid bone, the base of the cranium, and at the ears or temporal bones. These places are addressed in the ten-step protocols because they are common sites of tension.

An important role of fascia is to accommodate the many internal and external forces that are placed upon the body. It holds us together—literally keeping our insides from falling out—while still allowing us to move freely. For example, consider the large external forces absorbed by the body in a car accident; it takes a remarkably resilient and adaptable body to recover from such extreme impacts. As for internal forces, they can be from a bacterial or viral infection or from an *emotional holding*, which is something that is created when emotions during a significant event are not fully felt and experienced. Maybe we were in danger and there was no time to acknowledge and process our feelings, or we were overwhelmed and chose to ignore it, but in any case we put the emotions "on hold" in a place in our bodies, to be dealt with later. There can also be incidents where there are both external and internal forces at work, such as a traumatic accident with a strong emotional component.

If we are vibrant and healthy and our fascia is supple and resilient, we can recover from incidents without much trouble. We experience pain and discomfort when our ability to adapt to these forces lessens; it's as if we start to run out of options. When we can't address life events as they happen, we hold their impacts in layers in the fascial structure, and these holdings take effort and energy to maintain. Then one seemingly small event, such as a quick turn of the head or bending to get something off the floor, can be the "straw that broke the camel's back" and tip the body into a downward spiral.

Fascial restrictions *in* the body can be felt from anywhere else *on* the body, much the same way the CSR can. During a CST session, we place our hands on the client in the same places we feel the CSR, and let our hands sink gently into the fascia. We then add a very slight pull, or drag, which adds a line of tension that we follow to see how far up the body it can travel. This technique is called *fascial glide*.

For example, say I have my hands on a client's ankles and add a five-gram downward drag to the fascia. I can't feel beyond the left knee with my left-side hand, but with my right-side hand I can feel beyond the right hip. This lets me know there is a fascial restriction at the level of the left knee and that everything is running smoothly in the right leg.

Just as I could feel increasing subtleties in the CSR as I gained more experience and developed my technique, so it is with fascial evaluation. Once I feel an area of restriction, I can place my hands there and feel into the fascia to identify more precisely where the problem is.

Every time I place my hands on areas of fascial restriction, the fascia has the opportunity to realign itself in a more functional way. When I work, my hands are "listening" and following the body's innate knowing of how this realignment should happen. The result is a more even line of tension along the body's length, as opposed to there being a lot of tension or stretch in any one area.

♡

A single fascial restriction can affect many other areas in the body. Take, for example, my client Maya. She developed intense left knee pain after walking down a steep hill, then began to experience pain in that knee after any strenuous exercise. She came to me for her very first CST session and was somewhat unsure about it, as she had never enjoyed receiving massages. I explained the process and asked her my usual questions before we got started. She told me she'd had only one surgery before, on her thyroid, five years ago.

I checked in with her CSR and felt a decreased amplitude in the rhythm as well as fascial restriction on the left side of her pelvis. She didn't have any pain in her pelvis and was perplexed as to why I started treatment there. As my hands started to connect with the tissue, however, Maya suddenly remembered that she'd had a hernia repair in that area. Her knee pain increased as the scar tissue softened under my hands, and she started to feel the connection between her pelvis and knee.

Next I worked on her sacrum and coccyx (tailbone). As I worked with her coccyx I could feel a lot of tension and holding. I asked her if she remembered anything happening in this area, perhaps a fall. She then recalled having part of her coccyx removed after giving birth—yet another surgery she'd forgotten! Again, her knee pain increased as I worked on this area.

By this time, Maya had started to relax and feel that this therapy might help her. I then placed my hands above and below the site of her thyroid surgery. Once again, she felt a response in her left knee. She began laughing, delighted at how her body was letting her know how everything is interconnected. Since that one treatment, Maya has had no knee pain.

Energy Cysts and Arcing

Another common evaluation technique besides fascial glide is *arcing,* which is used to identify where the energy of trauma—whether physical, chemical, or emotional—is being held in the body. The body tries to minimize the disruption of traumatic energy by containing it in a specific area. Compressing this foreign, disorganized energy into a small space creates a "cyst" of energy. Although doing so is less disruptive and dangerous than allowing the energy to move freely throughout the body, the presence of such cysts still interferes with the body's function and disrupts the CSR.

Think of a river: the water flows around any stones or debris that are in its way, and there will be an obvious increase in turbulence if there are any large barriers in the river. Just as it is difficult to keep our balance in rough waters when we're swimming or kayaking, it is hard for the body to stay in balance if there are places that are unable to flow with ease.

Arcing is the tool that differed most from anything I'd learned in my physical therapy training. *Energy cysts* exhibit a characteristic arclike signature that is different from the motion of the CSR. These arcs of energy are centered on the cyst, and palpating allows us to locate them more precisely. As I have become more practiced, I can identify very accurately where energy cysts are in the body.

Releasing Energy Cysts

One technique for dealing with energy cysts is similar to that which is used with fascial diaphragms in the ten-step protocols: the therapist places a hand on either side of the cyst and engages with the tissue, following its movement as it normalizes. Another is called *unwinding.* This method involves supporting a limb in which an energy cyst has been identified and allowing for spontaneous release to happen.

When I am supporting an arm or leg as it unwinds, I am also monitoring changes in the tissue under my hands and paying close attention to the CSR. Sometimes the motions the body makes will speed up, "skipping over" important places and thereby passing up an opportunity to fully release a restriction. I feel the CSR stop briefly and then come back on again, a sensation similar to listening to a CD as it skips over part of a song. At these moments, I intentionally slow down the movement slightly, without controlling where it goes. During release, the CSR will often stop, showing that significant work is happening in the body. Then, once the energy cyst is released, the CSR returns and the limb will stop its movement and relax.

By paying close attention to what is happening in the body in this manner, a therapist is able to work effectively with some of the more subtle and hidden ways in which the body holds on to patterns that are no longer helpful.

Evaluation Techniques and Going Beyond the Protocols

Traditional physical evaluations often miss the mark because the human structure is complex and we adapt to life events in myriad unique ways. When other therapy techniques have failed to fully resolve an issue, the three evaluation tools of CST (feeling the CSR, fascial glide, and arcing) can provide a quick and accurate way to find the source of a problem.

For example, think back to the example of Maya and her knee pain. If her knee had been treated for soft tissue inflammation with the traditional application of ice, elevation, and rest, her symptoms would have subsided in the short-term. However, this would have missed the related areas in her pelvis, coccyx, and thyroid that also contributed to her pain. Without the holistic approach of CST, treatment would not have cleared up the true reasons for her recurring knee pain.

Competent CST practitioners employ these three evaluation tools at the beginning of every session. After the assessment, the therapist has a clear picture of the client's status on that particular day, which helps to organize treatment and evaluate progress as the session continues. When I was still learning, my evaluation took quite a bit of time, but now I can usually do an assessment within two or three minutes.

Once I became confident with the evaluation tools and the techniques in both ten-step protocols, I was able to stop following the protocols step-by-step. Instead, CST sessions could be driven by the results of my evaluation, which showed me each client's most pressing issue in the moment. Although the protocols were very helpful when starting out, this is a more efficient way to work.

Dialoguing and SomatoEmotional Release

After receiving a thorough grounding in the basics of CST, I took classes on *SomatoEmotional Release* (SER) at the Upledger Institute. SER is, as one of my teachers, Tim Hutton, Ph.D., describes it, "the body's natural way of letting go of trauma from the tissue."

The body's tissues remember events by holding tension from the moment those events occurred. In the moment an accident happens, we often don't have time to pay attention to how our bodies are feeling. We wall off the sensations and emotions in our bodies; perhaps we think that we'll pay attention to them later, but we never do seem to get around to it. CST is a great way to reconnect to these stored emotions and tension.

SER is a phenomenon that occurs during a CST session. As the local tissue under a therapist's hand is responding and changing during therapy, there is a ripple effect out to other areas of the body. In other words, the entire body reacts and responds when work is being done in one area. There is often an emotional connection and a memory attached to the process, but that's not always the case.

When an SER is happening in the body, there is a complete stop in the CSR, which is called the *significance detector.* At the very moment that I register a stop in my client's CSR, the person often spontaneously says something like, "Do you think that you're working on what happened in that gymnastics accident I had when I was seven?" or "Wow, I was just thinking about the time I fell out of a tree and broke my arm—I haven't thought about that in years!"

Paying attention to the CSR and noting the significance detector helps us know when something important and beneficial is happening in therapy. I can support clients in their exploration of a memory as their tissues change; then, if I notice the CSR has resumed, I know that we are no longer in that particular therapeutic place.

Sometimes, when there is a deep stop in the rhythm signifying an emotional holding in the body, therapeutic verbal dialogue can help facilitate a more complete release. It can provide a deeper understanding of how a traumatic situation impacted us on a physical, emotional, and spiritual level. However, there are also times when it is not appropriate to have any verbal dialogue at all. These are usually times when a client is in a deep state of relaxation. Then, a conversation would have no therapeutic benefit or might even be a disruption to the process. At these moments, the inquisitive part of me that wants to know the story has to be put aside.

The skill of knowing what to say or, better yet, what *not* to say, is an art form and an ever-evolving process for me. Dr. John used a bold, direct style of dialoguing with his patients, which was an authentic place for him to work from, but which would sound odd coming from me. It was important for me to find my own authentic style of working and dialoguing. It seems that as long as you are being yourself, any style works—clients can always tell when somebody is being phony!

Therapeutic dialogue is *not* psychotherapy, and the degree and style to which therapists facilitate SER with dialogue depends on how experienced and comfortable they are with it. I deepened my skills through attending study groups, receiving and giving CST with a group of my colleagues, and getting further training in coaching skills. My years of experience and diligent practice also help me recognize when I have reached the limit of my professional capability and must refer patients to another professional, such as a psychotherapist.

CST on a Cellular Level

Dr. John was continuously doing research and expanding the field of CST. In 2003 he wrote an academically dense book called *Cell Talk,* in which he goes into incredible detail explaining how cells function, the roles of the different areas of the brain, and the intricacies of our immune system. The fun part for me was reading how current medical and academic information can be applied to CST. There are several classes based on this work at the Upledger Institute, each one focusing on a different aspect of the body, such as the brain or the immune system.

In one of the appendices of *Cell Talk,* Dr. John discusses *cellular memory,* the idea that cells have their own experience of life and can remember events that affect them. The concept of cellular memory may seem a little "out there," but I've found it to be very useful therapeutically. One of the most convincing stories I came across is from the book *The Heart's Code* by Paul Pearsall. In this book, Pearsall shares the story of an eight-year-old girl who received a heart from a murdered ten-year-old girl. The girl who received the heart started having vivid nightmares, recalling details of the murder. Her dreams were so specific, they were ultimately able to find and convict the other girl's murderer. Similar stories, though not always quite as dramatic, have been recounted by CST practitioners who have worked with transplant patients.

It's as though memories of experiences that have not been adequately addressed are stored in the cells of the body. These memories can surface when the person encounters a similar experience, but they can also surface when a person is using a healing modality such as CST, either while the person is undergoing therapy or sometimes a bit later. For example, during a CST session, one of my clients recalled being born prematurely. She felt so cold that she was shivering and trembling on my table. She had been born back when hospitals were just beginning to develop the knowledge and technology to support a premature baby, so she probably hadn't been kept adequately warm.

Feeling into the sensations and memories that show up during a session brings a deeper level of understanding and awareness to my clients. This can cause dramatic change, but it can just as commonly lead to a small, manageable step toward relieving pain in the body.

CST and the Immune System

While taking CST and the Immune Response, one of the classes based on *Cell Talk,* I was five months pregnant with my twins. Students practice on each other in every class, so we all have ample opportunity to be therapists and clients.

In one class session in which I was the client, I became aware of a flulike virus that was affecting one of my babies. I asked my body if it could take on that virus, as my immune system was more mature and able to mobilize to deal with it better than my baby's could. Amazingly, I then immediately felt every flulike symptom you can get! I was feverish and had an intense ache in my kidneys as well as one deep in my bones. My body's immune system quickly got to work, and within about five minutes all of my symptoms were gone. My experience may sound bizarre and improbable, but it's not uncommon—when you get such a felt sense in your body, there's no denying it.

This class helped us develop skills in working with bacterial, viral, and fungal infections in the body, and provided helpful tools for working with autoimmune disorders. In *Living Beyond Miracles,* Deepak Chopra talks about the immune system and describes the immune cells as "a roving nervous system." This analogy gives you some idea of the intelligence and the immensely complicated nature of how our immune system works. There is still a lot more to be scientifically explained, but CST can give practical, effective ways to work directly with this vital system.

CST and the Brain

Ever since learning neuroanatomy in college, I have had a fascination with how the brain functions. In another class based on *Cell Talk,* titled The Brain Speaks, we studied in depth the different structures of the brain and how they relate to each other.

We spent a good amount of time focusing on the cerebellum, a region at the base of the brain. It is crucial for coordinating our movements smoothly and, from an evolutionary standpoint, is one of the oldest parts of the brain. Whenever I work with the cerebellum I get the impression that I'm working with a wise elder who should command our respect, but who is often not listened to. However, once the cerebellum has our attention, a solution to the problem that affects it is quickly found.

The neocortex, the newest area of our brain to develop, is the region of our brain involved in conscious thought, among other things. It has a habit of overriding the cerebellum, and there is often a lack of communication between the two areas. This disconnect is reflected in our culture's tendency to have the rational, logical part of our brain dominate decision making. However, I believe that the cerebellum is happier once there are agreed lines of communication established between it and the neocortex. (My impressions have been confirmed by the experiences of many other craniosacral therapists.)

While in class, during another session in which I was the client, I had a revelation regarding the structure called the *fornix*. The fornix has a shape similar to a ram's horns and connects the hippocampus, the area that processes long-term memory, to other parts of the brain.

Interestingly, as the student acting as therapist contacted my fornix, I realized that I have a tendency to butt heads with people and "lock horns." This response was clearly ingrained into my memory system, and my brain and body presented a picture to my mind's eye of rams butting heads to resolve their conflicts. Somehow this had become a learned pattern of behavior that I had little awareness of. In that session I realized that I do not need to butt heads and that I can simply let go of my attachment to being right. It was a profound realization that also seemed to cause some kind of rewiring in my brain, as I was freed from this old pattern of behavior (for the most part!).

Another important structure of the brain is the reticular activating system, or reticular alarm system (RAS). It extends from below the brain stem up through the midbrain and thalamus. This system is what its name implies: our response to emergency. It puts us into fight-or-flight mode, and increases the amount of adrenaline in our bodies. This is an appropriate and necessary response to actual danger, but in the modern day we activate our RAS for stress and perceived threats, such as "I might lose my job" or "that driver cut me off!" This leads to an RAS that's chronically activated, which is exhausting for the body and depletes us of energy. Then our bodies don't have energy to heal from our everyday activities, much less old injuries and insults. Using CST, we can dialogue with the RAS, encouraging it to reset its everyday level of activation to a lower, more appropriate level. This has been incredibly useful for my clients as well as for me personally.

One tool that's good for giving the brain a little boost is called cranial pumping. This technique is done by following the CSR at the head and enhancing its motion there with a gentle pumping action. This gives a lift to the entire craniosacral system, and minor restrictions in the body resolve easily.

Deepening Understanding and Continuing Learning

The Upledger curriculum is continuously updated and additional classes are developed as new research comes out. For example, since I started, there are now classes on conception, pregnancy, and birthing; reversal of the aging process and the treatment of Alzheimer's and dementia; and working in the ocean with the help of dolphins. In recent years, additional research papers have been published that measured the CSR and looked at CST's effectiveness with diseases such as dementia, fibromyalgia, and multiple sclerosis. There is an extensive research library available on the Upledger Institute website, and the Institute is actively working toward gathering case studies to drive future research.

I continue to deepen my learning by attending and assisting with classes, as well as by meeting regularly with my *multihands* group of experienced craniosacral therapists. (A multihands session is a CST session in which more than one therapist works on a client at a time.) This group has met every few months for years, and we've even done a couple of weekend retreats together. We share case studies and experiences, and provide support and acknowledgment for each other's personal challenges and successes. Most of our time together is spent in session. The support of skilled and like-minded therapists is invaluable to me both personally and professionally, as I continue to develop my skills.

Dr. John believed that just about anyone can do CST, and so he opened up his beginning CST classes to everyone. (In keeping with this spirit, the Institute offers a one-day ShareCare class for anybody who would like to learn basic techniques to use on their loved ones. I share some of those ShareCare techniques at the end of this book.) The biggest benefit to Dr. John's openness is that this powerful work is now widely known and accessible to many people. The downside is that, since CST is not a licensed profession, there are varying levels of competency in therapists who claim to practice CST.

The advantage of having a licensed profession, like nursing or physical therapy, is that it provides the consumer with a basic level of protection, because licensing bodies ensure that their practitioners are meeting certain standards of practice and following a code of ethics. This is a costly process and, as it is done on a state-by-state basis, many states do not want to increase the types of licenses they are in charge of. Therefore, the Upledger Institute decided that it would be beneficial to therapists, clients, and the craniosacral therapy community as a whole to set its own internal standards, with two levels of certification.

The first level of certification, CranioSacral Therapy Techniques Certification, requires that a practitioner take certain classes and complete a comprehensive essay exam, an objective exam, and a hands-on practical/oral exam. The second level, CranioSacral Therapy Diplomate Certification, can be taken after earning Techniques Certification and then completing more advanced classes. It too has an essay exam, objective exam, and practical/oral exam. In addition, Diplomate candidates are required to perform five hours of talks or to publish an article, and then either intern at the Upledger Institute or take a Clinical Applications class, in which an advanced instructor observes their work over five days. I earned both certifications and have found that doing so helped me deepen my knowledge base and skill level in a way that would not be possible without the structure and accountability of the exams.

♡

From reading this chapter I hope you have a better sense of the "nuts and bolts" of CST, and of its potential to help you. I know that once you've experienced the therapy yourself, your understanding will deepen. In the next chapter, we will take a look at what you might experience in a typical session.

Chapter Three

What to Expect in a Session

Every CST session is unique. Each client has his or her own ways of processing emotions and energy, which can vary from day to day, and therapists have their own styles of working, too. However, the general structure typically stays the same, and in this chapter I will take you through a description of how sessions can unfold. Then we will explore case studies to give you an idea of how sessions vary based on individuals and circumstances.

The Initial Meeting: Building Trust

During a person's first visit with a craniosacral therapist, the session is usually spent becoming familiar with CST and building a level of rapport and trust. When I first meet clients I ask them questions as part of my intake process, which helps us get to know each other a little and gives me an idea of their expectations. One question I always ask is: "What results would you like from receiving CST?" My goal is to get the client to express his or her desires in measureable, concrete objectives.

For example, somebody might answer, "I want to be in less pain." If I follow up with the question, "How will you know that you are in less pain?" I might get an answer like, "When I don't have to take any painkillers during the day." This line of questioning helps us both get clear on not only what we want to achieve, but also what signs would indicate that we had achieved it.

During the intake procedure, an important process is being initiated that affects both parties. As my client and I are chatting, there is a conscious verbal dialogue going on, as well as nonverbal and nonconscious dialogues. This is due, in part, to cells in the brain called mirror neurons that help us understand the actions and intentions of other people. In a 2006 *New York Times* article, Dr. Giacomo Rizzolatti said, "We are exquisitely social creatures. Our survival depends on understanding the actions, intentions and emotions of others. Mirror neurons allow us to grasp the minds of others not through conceptual reasoning but through direct simulation. By feeling, not by thinking."

Mirror neurons underscore the importance of therapeutic presence during a session. One of the reasons I continue to receive frequent CST work and maintain a regular meditation and yoga practice is to stay grounded and neutral for my clients. I know that otherwise my clients' nonconscious awareness will pick up on my energy and they'll feel less safe, even if they couldn't explain exactly why.

After the first session, a client and therapist will typically know whether they're a good fit for each other. (I also like to check in with my clients about their goal after about three sessions; at that point, if we have not yet already achieved it, we should be making very good progress toward it.) Once a client and I have finished going over his or her history, and I know that it's safe to perform CST, the work of the session can begin.

CST Work in Session

As we begin, I generally ask clients if they have any questions for me, and encourage them to speak up at any time, especially if something is uncomfortable. I then ask them to lie on my treatment table, fully clothed and face up. Supports and cushions may be added for comfort. When clients cannot easily lie face up, such as during the later stages of pregnancy, they can lie on their sides instead. Children rarely stay still; luckily, that's not a requirement for a successful treatment. However, when treating children, agility may be required—another way that my yoga practice comes in handy!

Once a client is comfortable, I place my hands on his or her feet and work my way up to the cranium, paying attention to the craniosacral rhythm and noting any fascial tension and energy cysts. Using the information I gain during this assessment, I decide which areas in the body should take priority. Then I place my hands over the area that is most in need and connect with the tissue there. I pay attention to what I'm feeling, gently allowing the information to come up into my hands as opposed to my sinking in and searching for it. At the same time, I note how my own body is feeling by asking myself, "Is there any tension I can let go of? Am I at ease?"

Sometimes I concentrate on just one area of the body or a single line of tension, sometimes on many simultaneously. As my hands follow a line of tension or a holding, my client often feels a corresponding line of tightness, an area of discomfort, or even symptoms similar to the condition that caused the client to come in for help in the first place—for example, a person who came in for migraine relief may develop a headache during a session. Clients might also feel a sensation in their body that reminds them of a traumatic or unpleasant event in their life. All of these are signs of tension leaving the body, and lets me know that I am working with the source of the problem. However, if it's too disconcerting or feels like "too much," then I can lighten up or remove my hands altogether.

The energy of each session seems to have a wavelike motion. Picture a client's feelings as the rise of the wave; then as it breaks there is a moment where release or change is felt in the tissue, and the pain dissipates or a deeper understanding about that unpleasant event is gained. When the wave ebbs, there is a range of different sensations that he or she might feel, which can be useful to track and tell the therapist about as they come up.

As a session progresses I may ask that clients bring their attention to a specific place in the body, usually because I notice a sense of holding or tension there. Sometimes it takes bringing their attention (in addition to my own) to an area in order to induce a relaxation and release. I will also ask clients to go inside their bodies and remember when it was in full working order, to pay attention to what that felt like. Using their imagination to experience what each cell was like when it was functional and vibrant can cause a change in the body, often including a sense of release. When clients feel an impulse to move I encourage them to do so, as it allows the tissues to let go of tension they were holding. As my clients' bodies unwind, it is rather like untangling a knotted-up necklace, twisting it this way a little and rolling that way a bit to unravel its kinks.

There are times that I will direct people to pay attention to a particular area of the body, then after getting a little verbal feedback no further words seem necessary. At the end of that kind of session clients may slowly open their eyes, reorient themselves, and share something of their experience. They often say it's like going to an in-between place—not asleep, yet not fully awake. Of course, some people do fall asleep and are anxious to know if they snored!

Getting to a place of such deep relaxation and letting go can be surprising for people. My father-in-law, Jim, had a similar experience when he came to me for therapy after I had just opened my practice. He had tinnitus (ringing in the ears) from having been in the Royal Navy and spending many hours working underneath the deck of an aircraft carrier. Jim had never experienced anything like CST before, but was happy to give it a try since his wife had enjoyed and recommended it.

My treatment followed the ten-step protocol I described earlier. We worked in silence, and he seemed to be very relaxed. I remember noticing a tightness in his tentorium cerebelli, the fascial membrane that runs horizontally through the brain. I released it with a technique called "ear pull," which is nearly exactly what it sounds like!

When Jim sat up at the end of the treatment, he was in a place of amazement. He said it was the first time he had noticed a pause in his mind's inner chatter. (This is something that often happens in meditation as well; it's amazing to observe your own inner dialogue, but it's actually more important to pay attention to the silence between the chattering.) Then, a few days later, Jim found that his tinnitus was gone! He remained in complete remission for about five months before the symptoms began to come back, but it has never returned to its original severity.

Maintaining Awareness of Sensations

If you're feeling tense and uncomfortable during your CST session, then beneficial therapeutic change can't happen. I always encourage clients to speak up if something doesn't feel right, and I let them know that if they need space I will back off right away. This is an important ground rule in respecting a person and establishing trust. Also, when performing CST mouth work on first-time clients, I ensure that they know they can stop the procedure immediately with just a wave of their hand. You are always in control of the proceedings, and it is okay to stop or take a break if things feel overwhelming. At times you may feel less-than-pleasant sensations, but you should always be aware that you're in a safe, comfortable environment.

As a CST client, it is useful to pay attention to the feelings in your body and let your therapist know of any changes. By drawing your attention inward, you'll be able to identify when your body lets go of what it has been holding. The most common signs of a release are a long deep breath, a twitch in a limb, a feeling of warmth, and a pulsing sensation like a little heartbeat. However, it is all very personal and subjective, and clients have also described to me sensations such as: cold, tingling, shaking, zinging, sense of peace, wavy motion, spreading, softening, heaviness, and lightness. However you describe it, what is most important is that you track your evolving sensations throughout a session.

Many people have a hard time finding the words to describe the changes they feel, partly because they have never done it before and the sensations that arise are unique. With a little guidance, however, most clients get very adept at this. Telling your therapist what you feel as it occurs will heighten your own awareness of your body and allow your therapist to refine hand placement or connection, if necessary.

On the other hand, I have done many sessions in which not a word has been spoken, yet profound change has occurred. I once did a completely silent session with a person who had fractured multiple bones in his body in a go-kart accident. At the end of the session, he slowly opened his eyes, sat up, and said, "Wow . . . that was wild! I went through every part of the accident in slow motion."

Integrating the Work After a Session

Generally, there will be a few minutes at the end of the session when the actual "work" is done and the allotted time is not yet up. Clients usually take these moments to integrate the session and ready themselves to go back into the world. I have frequently been asked, "Do I have to get up now? Can't I just stay here for the rest of the day?" People have often told me that they went home afterward and took a nap or had a particularly good night's sleep.

It can be disorienting to open your eyes and sit up after being in a deep state of relaxation and inward attention, so take your time once the CST session is over. Look around the room slowly, and note how your body feels as you move. Is your posture different? Has your pain or discomfort changed? Do you feel lighter and more open? Allow yourself to simply feel these changes rather than dissect the session with your therapist. Analyzing has a tendency to take you away from your experiences on the table.

Case Study: Facial Paralysis

The following case study focuses on how people notice change not only physically and emotionally, but also spiritually, and gain a deeper understanding of their inner self. Although we were able to do only one CST session together, it was the catalyst for profound change in many areas of my client's life.

Nicollette was referred to me by Dr. Wayne Dyer (who also describes her story in his book *Wishes Fulfilled).* She'd recently been diagnosed with Bell's palsy, a condition in which the function of the seventh cranial nerve, or facial nerve, on one side of the face is inhibited. The facial nerve is what controls our expressions: smiling, frowning, opening and closing our eyelids. The cause of Bell's palsy is unknown, but it's thought to be related to exposure to a viral infection.

During our session, Nicollette and I discussed her condition. With the severe paralysis on the left side of her face, she was unable to close her left eye, and needed to tape it shut each night. She had trouble pronouncing words and chewing properly, and she couldn't taste with the left side of her tongue. She also had shooting pains in her head. Doctors had told her that she might never recover, and even if she did it could take years. This was devastating news, especially for a 20-year-old.

Since we were conducting therapy while on the beautiful island of Maui, I suggested that Nicollette pay attention to the sounds of the ocean. I also asked her to note any changes in sensation and notify me of them if she felt comfortable doing so. Then I gently placed my hands on her and evaluated her craniosacral rhythm. Noting fascial tension, an energy cyst, and diminishment of the

CSR at her diaphragm, I placed my hands over and under her rib cage on the left side and waited to see what her tissue wanted to do. There was a lot of tension in the muscles along either side of her spine, so much that her lower back could not rest on the bed. When my hands were drawn over her stomach, her CSR spontaneously stopped, which let me know that this place was therapeutically important.

I asked Nicollette if she noticed any sensations where my hands were or anywhere else in her body. She said she felt an increase in pressure from within her body and was having a vision of the color yellow in an oval shape. With my prompting she checked in with the yellow oval and asked what role or purpose it had. As she started to really pay attention and connect with this image, she described it bursting into a million pieces, floating all over her body. The yellow color became a part of her body, and she suddenly felt completely relaxed. As she absorbed these sensations, I could feel a softening and spreading of her tissue under my hands. The muscles along her spine let go, and her lower back was now able to rest on the bed.

At this point, there was more happening than just a marked change in my client's physical body. Linda, Nicollette's mother, was sitting in the room during the session as well. She described feeling a combination of peace and a heightened energy. She later said, "I recall at one point smiling because I was witnessing healing. I could see it, I could feel it!"

After placing my hands over Nicollette's collarbone and the base of her neck, I followed the movement of the tissue as it came to a balanced place. I worked on the area between the top of her neck and the base of her skull, which is a common place to hold tension. It can get quite sore as the deep layers of muscles here let go, but it's often described as a "good hurt." When I work with this area, I guide clients in concentrating on their breath and imagining tension leaving their body with each exhale. It is vital to get the tissues in the neck as relaxed as possible before working with the head, because there are major blood vessels and lymphatic structures running through this area and there needs to be an easy flow of fluids in and out of the brain when areas here are released.

I could feel that Nicollette's sphenoid was pulled in a way that implied it had sustained a direct blow. This butterfly-shaped bone forms the back of the eye sockets; the outside edges can be felt at our temples. Since it's right in the middle of our heads, it has sutures with many other bones of the cranium, and its smooth functioning can help the entire craniosacral system. Nicollette was shocked when I asked if she had hit her head. She replied, "Come to think of it, yes! I did bang my head on the car door when I was rushing to get to the airport. How did you know that?"

I then put on a glove so I could feel inside Nicollette's mouth. I could tell that the maxilla, the roof of her mouth, was restricted, and I used my fingers to follow its unwinding motion. I also noticed that her vomer, a thin bone running along the center of the mouth, was pulling to one side, reflecting and creating imbalance in the whole system. As I gently worked with the vomer, I felt it move and come back to the centerline. Nicollette's sphenoid regained normal motion and her CSR became smooth and balanced.

Toward the end of the session, I asked Nicollette to picture what a representation of healing would look like for her. She arrived at an image of a sponge filled with a pale blue light. We called this healing blue light into her body, envisioning a sponge soaking it up. Nicollette then took a deep breath, and I felt her whole body go into a state of profound relaxation.

I ended the session by inducing a still point at her occiput to help her nervous system relax even more and support her body in making its self-corrections. As she got up, Nicollette mentioned that she'd lost the concept of linear time and the session was a bit of a blur—common observations in CST work. She later told me that she'd almost expected to be able to smile when the session ended. Although she was a little disappointed that this wasn't the case, she still felt a deep sense of peace.

Reflecting after her session, Nicollette said, "After that experience I would say that you helped me realize the control I have over my body. You helped me jump-start the communication between my mind and my body. I was introduced to the notion of how my mind and body are one."

Ongoing Effects

Nicollette eventually made a complete physical recovery. Her body was no longer spending a significant amount of energy holding on to the fear of whether she would regain normal muscle control of her face, which left plenty of energy for many positive changes in her life. It was a joy to see how these experiences impacted Nicollette once she left Maui. Linda called to tell me that the experience of having worked with Dr. Dyer and me had impacted them both deeply. Her daughter was now focusing her energy on what she wanted and on the feeling of already having achieved it as opposed to dwelling on what she did not want.

As a woman just embarking on her adult life, Nicollette has used this experience to empower herself. Some changes have been relatively simple—for example, learning to play golf. She had always wanted to learn how to play, and the next thing she knew she had gotten a job at a golf course with free lessons. More profound changes that have affected the course of her life include Dr. Dyer inviting Nicollette onstage several times during his speaking tours to share her experience. After each talk, she was swamped by people who were moved and inspired by her story. After being asked to speak at several events, she is now considering making public speaking part of her future career.

Case Study: Working with the Family

The following story demonstrates some of the adaptations that come with working with young children and babies. You'll get a sense of what to expect with this age group and the changes that occur over several sessions, as opposed to the single session that Nicollette received. We'll also explore how CST's impact extends beyond the energetic changes of the body to create positive changes in the whole family system.

Meeting Mark

When I met Mark at our initial consultation, he was a delightful 15-month-old boy. His mother, Annie, told me that he had recently begun having seizures several times a day, and would be going to a pediatric neurologist soon for a diagnosis. Mark had Down syndrome, but he'd been hitting all of his developmental milestones until the past six months when his overall development slowed, and he was now showing significant delay in all areas. Annie also mentioned that Mark had needed a number of invasive medical interventions on his mouth and throat shortly after his birth. With my years of experience as a pediatric physical therapist, working in hospitals and with children with special needs, I was able to bring much of my background, in addition to my CST skills, to bear in Mark's case.

When I began my assessment, I noticed that Mark's sacrum had very little motion and the base of his cranium was very tight. I placed my hands above and below his sacrum and felt it slowly release and soften with some heat released from the tissues. I also felt tight areas along the length of his spine release and lengthen.

Mark began to cry when my hands moved to the right side of his neck. Crying isn't a cause for alarm; it's simply how preverbal children convey their emotions. I need to monitor the CSR carefully when babies start to cry because if the CSR stops, this lets me know that they are in their process and expressing how they are feeling. This can sometimes be challenging, as both therapist and parent instinctively want to reach out and soothe the crying!

I explained to Annie that I was not hurting Mark, and described how his body was letting go of tension. I also reinforced to her that if she wanted me to stop at any time, I would do so immediately. It was especially important for Annie to feel in control during our sessions because she had felt so powerless while witnessing Mark undergo painful medical procedures. I stopped work several times, which is common when working with young children; it paces the session in a way that is less overwhelming and allows them to get a few reassuring cuddles from their parent.

At the end of our first session together I was able to get some opening at the base of Mark's cranium by gently placing my fingers on the muscles there and holding a clear intention. I went very lightly in this delicate area of the body, using my mind's eye to picture the structure that I wished to release and using the light touch of my fingertips to monitor changes in the tissue below. I made a few adaptations to standard CST techniques, as the bony structure is still maturing in an infant, and with Mark's Down syndrome his structure would likely be even less stable.

Annie and I both noticed that Mark was able to sit with a straighter spine by the end of the first session. The improvement when he got home was much more astounding. As she described it, "The evening after his first session with Kate, Mark crawled for the first time. More precisely, Mark had never before attempted to crawl, and that evening he was crawling back and forth between Mom and Dad with speed and vigor. We were beyond ecstatic. He was on no medications of any kind; the only change in his treatment had been CST."

It's a major shift in children's development when they realize they can move toward a place they want to go and no longer need to rely on a caregiver to get a toy for them (or to get up to some mischief!). Independent mobility demonstrates an awakening of the internal drive to explore your environment, and it's stimulating for all areas of development.

Continuing Sessions

By his second visit, Mark had been diagnosed with seizures and started on medication. I worked on freeing up the sacrum some more and could feel lengthening through both the sacrum and coccyx. To help Mark integrate this new freedom of movement

I used a technique called *rock and glide,* which mobilizes the whole dural tube. I put one hand under his cranium and the other under his sacrum, then followed the CSR up and down the length of his spine, helping mobilize it and free any restrictions. This is a very soothing technique to have done as an adult as well; it feels like you are being rocked and fully supported.

Mark fell asleep during treatment and stayed asleep for the rest of the session. Annie was happy, as her son had been unable to take a nap since he'd started his seizure medication and was constantly tired and cranky. I was able to continue work while he slept, and felt a further opening through his respiratory diaphragm. Mark was carried out to the car asleep and continued his nap in his car seat.

In the next session, we worked on freeing up the structures around Mark's upper chest and throat. The area involved strong emotions for both Mark and Annie, and he quickly became agitated. This prompted Annie to share a story about a doctor's visit in which they had used an anesthetic spray to look down her son's throat; he'd had a severe reaction to the procedure and choked. She recalled the panic of the clinic staff and how powerless she felt because she could only sit there and watch.

Telling the story in my office, Annie finally had the space and time to acknowledge how hard it had been. She allowed herself to feel the complex mix of emotions from that time and shed some of the tears that were held back. She had been unable to reach out and hold her son as she'd wanted, because the medical staff had been so busy treating him. Now she expressed her desire to find her voice and learn to speak up for Mark.

On their next visit Annie noted that Mark had become a lot more vocal, was more interactive with his older brother and sister, and had progressed from "commando crawling" to crawling on his hands and knees. When he came in and sat on the table, he made good eye contact with his beautiful, twinkling green eyes.

As we continued CST work on his neck, throat, and mouth, Annie talked about a difficult time Mark had with breathing when he was around six months old. He had an episode of croup, and his doctor spent one visit repeatedly scooping mucus out of Mark's mouth and throat. She also mentioned that Mark had been born with the umbilical cord around his neck—yet another layer of trauma in the soft tissue of the throat. It made sense that he'd been having trouble vocalizing and was now having issues with eating and the texture of his food; he was understandably very sensitive to anything coming near his mouth. His oral hypersensitivity started to lessen as I gently worked on the different structures in his mouth.

While Mark was receiving CST, Annie felt empowered to become more active in his medical treatment. She researched different ways to treat seizures and became an active participant in various online support groups. Based on her studies, Annie took Mark to a DAN! doctor, which is one who uses the "Defeat Autism Now" protocol of the Autism Research Institute. This doctor discovered high levels of lead and mercury in Mark's blood, so they started treatment to clear these heavy metals out of his system. Annie later told me, "You showed me what a grounded, intelligent, intuitive, strong, independent-thinking, humble woman is. I learned so much from what you told me, but even more from just watching you work."

CST for Mom

I also did one CST session with Annie herself. Since Mark had been born, it had been one life-threatening situation after another for him, and she had been spending most of her time in survival mode. She'd had very little time to process and feel the strong emotions she had gone through.

As I discussed in the last chapter, our reticular alarm system (RAS) can be set on high when we repeatedly experience ourselves as being in danger. Annie was in a constant state of alert and unable to dial down her RAS. This changed after working with me.

Annie was deeply affected by her CST session. She had a vision of a gray fist, which represented a harsh, self-critical, and judgmental voice. She sensed that this voice had far too much influence and power over her, and as she talked and negotiated with the fist, it eventually faded away and dissolved. I'd been holding my hands above and below her navel as she dialogued with the fist, and I could feel the tension in the tissue soften as she came to a resolution. Afterward she told me, "I have never experienced anything like that, even in meditation. It was really life changing. The voice comes back to make me feel bad, but it no longer has any authority, and it just doesn't penetrate." I felt like a single session with Annie did as much good as five sessions of work with Mark, because it helped her reduce self-doubt and feel empowered to make choices for him

When working with children, it can be very important for the mother to receive CST, too. Mothers are often central to the smooth running of a family. If the mother is well taken care of, the whole family system is better off. Ironically, many mothers have a hard time making themselves a priority and would rather concentrate all their efforts on their child. However, as I mentioned earlier, the state of a mother's nervous system is always felt and responded to by her children. The calmer the mother's nervous system, the calmer everybody is!

Results

After I did ten CST sessions on Mark (and one on Annie), the family moved to the East Coast, but I hear about Mark regularly. The family continues to combine allopathic and alternative treatments, and they're seeing slow and steady improvements. Annie recently described Mark this way: "He is a smiling, crawling, clapping—and most important, happy—little four-year-old. He does not speak with words or signs yet, but I can read his eyes." However, the path of healing isn't always smooth. There are periods when Mark has no seizures, but he also once had one so severe that he was hospitalized.

Annie offered this description of her CST experience and results: "Kate worked with Mark and the results were quite fascinating. He was usually wary of new people and generally uninterested in his surroundings, yet he took an immediate liking to Kate. He made eye contact with her, snuggled with her, and communicated with her on a very deep, nonverbal level. He does not display this behavior with his physical or occupational therapists.

"Mark worked through many obstacles with Kate. The seizures made him unable to sleep, so he was often restless yet exhausted. On days of CST, he would become calm and grounded. I could always depend on a good nap after these sessions, and good naps at that time were precious gems!

"On my own personal note, Kate has opened my eyes to many different treatment options for him; these alternative treatments have proven *extremely* beneficial for him, and I have only her to thank.

"To be sure, without Kate in our lives, this mommy and baby would be lost in an abyss of unsuccessful medications and an absence of options. She has restored my hope and steadied my emotions many times."

♡

You'll note that in many of the sessions I described, I asked my clients questions as the session progressed. I wondered aloud what healing would be like for them and asked them what their body knows or needs. In the next chapter, I describe in depth another important tenet of CST: it helps people access and communicate with their own self-healing mechanisms. We call this "accessing the inner wisdom," or, as Dr. John called it, the "inner physician."

From working with so many clients over the last decade, I know that some of you will be very comfortable with this idea, while for others it will feel totally alien. Just know that sessions can also be successful when performed in complete silence, and that when the situation is right, contacting your inner wisdom directly can support profound change.

Chapter Four

Accessing and Using Your Inner Wisdom

A fundamental premise of craniosacral therapy is that the body knows how to heal itself. However, while this knowledge is held within each of us, it doesn't mean that accessing this information is always easy. We often need support to reach our inner wisdom, to allow us to move beyond our logical or rational minds.

As Albert Einstein is thought to have said, "Problems cannot be solved at the same level of awareness that created them." We've all had the experience of running a scenario over and over in our heads, thinking up different possible courses of action, with none seeming to do the trick. Can you recall what this feels like in your body? I know that going through this process leaves me feeling like a hamster on a wheel, overwhelmed and exhausted.

When you access your inner wisdom, particularly in a CST session, you can find solutions that hadn't seemed possible before. Your active participation and the back-and-forth dialogue with your therapist can open up new experiences for you. Don't get stuck in the mind-set of: "I pay you, then I lie down and you fix me." The greatest healing and most illuminating discoveries happen when clients explore their body's wisdom in partnership with their therapist.

Some people are overly self-reliant and have a hard time turning to a therapist for support, thinking they need to go it alone. Many are raised with the belief that they need to solve their problems themselves, that it is a sign of weakness to ask for help. Others feel that they are being disloyal if they talk to anyone about their relationship difficulties. In Britain, there is the cultural norm to "keep a stiff upper lip." In America, the pioneer spirit runs deep, and Americans tend to think that nearly everything should be done on their own.

Although a good self-help practice is essential to a healthy life (and I will elaborate on some examples in a later chapter), we must recognize when it is essential to seek aid. We are all interconnected, and support is a critical part of our healing process; when we are open to help, our issues can be resolved much more quickly. CST is an excellent way for us to give and receive assistance. In addition to the support given by a therapist, inviting your body's knowledge into a session will add that extra care you need.

Accessing Your Inner Wisdom

When introducing the concept of inner wisdom to clients, I ask whether it makes sense to them that we each have a part of us that is aware of all that goes on in our bodies and lives. For many people, it is not a big stretch to accept that they do have this inner knowing, although some doubt their ability to reach it. Once they've acknowledged the existence of their inner wisdom, I ask whether they would like to use it to help guide us in our session. People often feel a sense of deep relaxation while undergoing CST, which makes it much easier to access their inner knowing. If they do not naturally drop into a state of ease, I can facilitate it by inducing a still point.

My clients have described their inner wisdom as taking various shapes, including angels, animals, spirit guides, the Holy Spirit, and other people (living or deceased). It seems to me that there is no limit to the forms that the body can use in order to communicate its knowledge. Once people are able to envision their inner wisdom, they can use this same approach to connect to a specific part of their body, such as their heart, and find out what it knows about a specific issue or how it's being affected.

Some people are happy to share everything they think and feel during a session, while others remain silent, sometimes doubting what shows up for them and worrying that they're not doing it right. As clients attempt to connect with their inner wisdom I continue to track their CSR, because I know it signifies something important if it comes to a halt. Often, my asking, "What happened just then?" is enough to encourage clients to begin sharing their experiences. Some people keep silent because they can't make any sense of their thoughts and feelings; however, some of the most profound discoveries I've witnessed have started with, "This makes no sense, but . . ."

Clients sometimes ask, "Do you know what I'm thinking? What do you see?" Honestly, I have no idea what they're thinking, and most of the time I don't see much! It's also not advised for CST practitioners to share any visions or knowledge that comes to us, as there is simply no way of knowing whether that information that comes to the therapist's mind is actually the clients' or their own.

Even if I were to receive accurate visions, it's more important for clients to access this knowledge themselves, in their own time, so they can trust and own it as their experience. I believe it is so important for all people to discover their own inner landscapes, their own answers, and their own ways of accessing their inner wisdom. This is why I sometimes ask my clients questions with the caveat that they should not feel compelled to answer them out loud. Also, on occasion, if my attention is drawn to a certain part of the body, I will suggest that they check in with themselves there. Although they may not notice anything at the time, often just the act of bringing their attention to an area is enough to effect change.

Communicating with Inner Wisdom

Once clients make contact with their inner wisdom, in whatever form it takes, I ask for permission to speak to it. If this is granted, I then ask that my clients allow it to speak without censoring or editing what it has to say. When we've reached this agreement, I begin asking questions about what is going on for my clients; then their inner knowing really directs the session from this point on.

Sometimes we are able to explore the origins of problematic dynamics. As an example, the creation of an energetic shield over your heart in early childhood would have been a beneficial method of protection then, but you find that later in life, instead of aiding you, this keeps you from connecting deeply with those you love. It can be important to acknowledge how something that now limits us had served us in the past; often, this acknowledgment aids the body in releasing what it is holding on to. While it is tempting to skip this step of exploring the meaning of troublesome sensations because we are eager to just be rid of them, we must not ignore this opportunity. After all, as Dr. John once said, "What we resist persists."

Protective mechanisms that have been set up in the body can be very reluctant to let go; your inner wisdom may be concerned as to how you'll deal with upcoming situations without the structures it has set in place to protect you. This resistance to change is something to respect, not avoid or try to change. Work in whatever way serves your highest and best interests.

As a client, the more CST work you receive and the more comfortable you are accessing your inner wisdom, the more you'll know when dialoguing with it is helpful and when you need to listen and be still. You may find that a meditation practice helps you get into a state of relaxation that supports accessing this part of yourself. You might also find this place in prayer, or while doing work with angels or spirit guides.

However, there are times when clients just cannot drop into that relaxed place where it is easier to access their inner knowing. In such situations I can monitor their CSR and use it to communicate with their body's wisdom through yes-or-no questions. I can ask questions out loud so that clients can hear them, or I can conduct the discourse silently—it's solely a matter of preference.

♡

Jane came to me not long after having had a brain tumor removed. She was preparing for a series of radiation treatments and was understandably nervous. After my assessment, I decided to begin at her thymus gland, a central figure in the immune system, to see how it could help handle the effects of the radiation. I asked Jane how she would prefer to work, and she chose asking questions out loud.

With my hand over the thymus, I asked, "Thymus—are you there?"

I felt Jane's CSR stop, indicating *yes.*

I continued, "Would it be okay to ask you some questions?"

Yes.

"Are you aware that Jane is undergoing radiation treatments for the remaining pieces of tumor in her brain?"

At this question, Jane's CSR did not stop, which indicated *no.* So I gave the thymus an explanation of the radiation treatment plan and schedule. Then I placed my other hand over Jane's head and asked, "Can you send some scout cells to check out the tumor that's still in this area?"

Yes.

The conversation went back and forth in this manner, and by the end of our session the areas that contained remnants of tumor cells felt a lot softer.

Jane sensed that this dialogue with her body helped prepare the healthy surrounding tissue for the radiation. She visualized how she wanted her treatment to go, picturing the cells in her body working in conjunction with the radiation and holding the belief that she would experience none of the predicted side effects. She continued her visualizations when she went in for treatments, and indeed, her radiation went smoothly, and she experienced no ill effects.

Mastering the Art of Dialogue

I learned how to dialogue with clients' inner wisdom through my classes at the Upledger Institute, and continue to develop my skills today. Being part of my multihands group has been invaluable because I not only get to practice with colleagues, but when I am on the receiving end I am provided with firsthand information on what works for me as a client. All the therapists I know continue to learn new ways of engaging in neutral, effective dialogue. To that end, I know one therapist who finds her experience with improvisational theater to be useful because it discourages holding an agenda or leading a dialogue, and encourages staying in the moment. She says it keeps her open to what the client is actually saying rather than focusing on her own ideas of what is happening.

I was able to continue refining my dialogue skills through my training in a technique called the *Inquiry Process*. I feel that this method deepened and bolstered the framework I learned at the Upledger Institute, giving me more tools to support clients as sensations, memories, or images surface in a session. After taking my first workshop, "Life Coaching for Results: An Introduction to the Inquiry Process," I decided to continue studying intensively with the founder, Amaran Tarnoff, for another three years.

In an intriguing example of synchronicity, the workshop first came to my attention after my husband returned from a business trip and announced that I should become a life-skills coach!

He'd been sitting next to a life coach on his return flight, and she had told him all about it. He had noticed that my friends would often seek me out to talk through their issues, and he knew that I enjoyed supporting them. I had never heard of life coaching, but given his conviction I investigated it more and came across Amaran and the Inquiry Process.

Amaran distilled the essence of his work into four steps, which sound deceptively simple, but hold great power once they're mastered.

The following is a brief description of how I use each step in my CST practice rather than a full explanation of the process, but it will give you a way to conceptualize how I work when dialoguing with others' inner wisdom. Applying the steps to your own life may even help you in your everyday relationships; it certainly did for me.

1. **Identify the result.** My clients and I begin by working together to get clear on what they expect to achieve through dialogue with their inner wisdom. We may also discover what a part of their body or mind needs to feel better; for instance, their heart may wish to be more open or to ache less.

2. **Discover the issue.** This is where the fun is! This is when my clients and I explore how an unhelpful pattern got set up in their body. This is commonly a period of negotiation with a client, because often a client wants the pain to leave *immediately* while the pain thinks it's needed and wants to stay! We find a middle ground by getting an understanding of each player's perspective: I act as an advocate for both my client and also the part that is holding on to the pain.

3. **Create a management strategy.** Once we've resolved what the main issue is, we can develop an action plan for dealing with it. For example, we might get the pain to agree to leave once the client commits to a meditation and yoga practice.

4. **Create a support strategy.** The final step is to set up nonjudgmental accountability for my clients, which can be as simple as telling a trusted friend when steps in the management strategy are completed, or committing to giving themselves a series of rewards for completing certain actions.

Framing the Dialogue

Through my training in the Inquiry Process, I learned how better to ask open-ended questions, those that can't be answered with a simple yes or no. I also practiced crafting nonjudgmental questions, as the act of being nonjudgmental is a fundamental principle within both CST and Inquiry Process teachings. People have a tendency to shut down when they feel that they are being judged, which reduces their ability to access solutions outside the realm of their everyday thinking.

Feeling safe helps us access our inner wisdom and listen to the intuitive, right side of our brain rather than our analytical left side. And when we monitor our own inner dialogue—or, as Amaran calls it, our "private conversation"—it may come as a surprise how much of our day is spent harshly judging ourselves. We rack our brains with "Why didn't I . . . ?" and "Why can't I . . . ?" I tell clients that "why" questions like these are often judgmental and get us no closer to solutions. I then guide them in finding an alternative way of framing such questions.

No matter how skillfully done, the whole dialogue process can sometimes feel like we're fumbling along in the dark. Regardless of my training and my best efforts to not be leading or judgmental, I still don't always frame questions in the most ideal way. However, many clients have their own performance anxiety about answering questions, too! As long as we remain in a therapeutic space, the session will still progress. I also like to remind clients that we are "playing with the edges here," looking for solutions not in our everyday awareness.

The Inquiry Process taught me to be comfortable with not knowing; in fact, I discovered that "not knowing" can be a very helpful place to be for a while. As Amaran once said, "People already have the answers. What is missing are the questions." Answers arise in their own timing, when the conditions are right. I'm no longer anxious when clients say "I don't know" to my questions; instead, I encourage them to be in that space of not knowing for a while, then check in periodically. I work with my clients to create the right conditions for answers to reveal themselves. Sometimes everything can be resolved while on the table, but this process can also continue between sessions.

Therapeutic Presence

Another key element to successfully working with the inner wisdom is the practitioner's therapeutic presence. When a client is working through something that touches me in a deep way, then I must be particularly mindful of how I am feeling and what is happening in my body. After my training at the Upledger Institute, I studied further under Suzanne Scurlock-Durana, a craniosacral therapist who trained directly with Dr. John before going on to develop a support system for therapists.

Suzanne created the Healing from the Core training program because she recognized the need to train therapists how to take care of themselves and not get depleted by their work. Her book, *Full Body Presence,* teaches how to maintain healthy therapeutic boundaries and how to stay aware of your body as you work. This practice of being present in your body helps you notice when you become ungrounded, and it is a useful tool for staying present with uncomfortable experiences.

Suzanne's book and CDs are as useful for clients as they are for therapists. Developing these skills can help you in your everyday life, as well as allow you to gain more from your CST sessions, by supporting you in staying present with feelings and situations you would otherwise avoid.

It takes skill for a therapist to be present with clients and not get sucked into their upset. Often, others' emotions trigger something unresolved in ourselves; or we may have the mistaken notion that we need to "fix" them. Once we get sucked in, we are no longer a useful therapeutic presence for the person on the table. It's draining for the therapist, and clients don't have the opportunity to look deeply at their own issues if their therapist needs support.

Case Study: Discovering an Inner Landscape

Developing tools to access our inner wisdom during a CST session can also give us a useful way to check in with ourselves in our everyday lives. In this case study, you'll see how my client continued to use the results of her dialogue as a self-help tool at home.

Kim is a client with whom I've worked for almost two years. During one of our sessions, she described how her self-esteem had been at an all-time low during her divorce from her first husband. She spoke in a matter-of-fact tone, as if it were an old issue and everything had been resolved long ago. And, to a large extent, it had been: she'd received counseling and she understood intellectually what had gone wrong in the marriage. However, there was a missing piece she was still holding in her body, because when we analyze with our rational minds we miss out on an important step in the healing process—feeling. It is as if our intellect considers itself superior to sensation and stops us from fully releasing the past.

As Kim and I worked together I encouraged her to note what was happening in her body as she talked, and I let her know what I was noticing as well. Then, in order to aid in her relaxation and sense of support, I asked her to picture a place or person that brought her peace. Kim quickly saw herself in a garden with her grandmother, surrounded by her love. The garden in her mind's eye consisted of flowers that had special meaning to her, all in white. Kim also noticed a veil behind the garden that separated her from what she felt were globes of energy. Each represented an issue that she knew needed attention, but which she kept at bay because she was afraid of dealing with them.

As Kim described the garden to me, I noticed that her craniosacral rhythm was off, indicating that our dialogue was of therapeutic value. My hands on Kim's stomach gave her a sense of physical connection, and my verbal encouragement added enough support that she felt able to look at the globes of energy.

Here is how Kim described working with two of the globes:

"The first globe is about my father's death. I was the sole caretaker during his brief illness, a terminal brain tumor. We had discussed his last wishes early on, and how he wanted things to be handled. I dove in with all my energy to assure him that everything he wanted was done. In the end I believed I had accomplished this, but after some time I began to wonder if *he* felt that I had. With the limited communication we had toward the end, I didn't receive this acknowledgement from him, so I started doubting myself. Along with the grief, this doubt has weighed on my mind for the last 18 years.

"Then I could see myself surrounded by these beautiful flowers in my garden, picking apart my doubts along with the events of those seven months. In my internal garden I can answer my doubts, and I do believe that I met my father's expectations and fulfilled his last wishes. Now when I see the garden in my mind's eye the globe is a brightly lit orb; I can feel love and brightness.

"The second issue is one I have been carrying for nearly 40 years. I married a wonderful person when I was very young, but I know now that I wasn't ready for the intensity of the love I felt. I was afraid I wasn't good enough for him, so I ran. When I took the plunge into exploring this second globe of pain and confusion, the garden I saw around me held the flowers that were in my bridal bouquet. This took a bit of time to interpret, but then it made sense to me: the core of the matter was to forgive myself for my immature actions.

"It was like a dam had broken, and all the emotions and answers filled my head. My heart once again felt the pain and humiliation I caused, but along with it came understanding and compassion for the young person I was then. Today I can view this situation more easily, but I still experience sadness for the young girl who was so unable to cope, so fearful of something wonderful.

"Although I covet that love, I still feel it today. I recognize now that I draw from this same pool of love when I care for others. I know that I can use this never-ending source of compassion in my everyday life, and in this way share the goodness of what was."

The garden became a familiar and safe place for Kim to go during our CST sessions in order to access her inner wisdom. Now it has become a regular practice for Kim at home, too, and is a quick and easy way for her to spend some quiet time with herself and to check in on how she's doing.

As you can see, there is no predicting how a session will unfold or how clients' problems and concerns will resolve. But when we trust in the process and our inner wisdom, the work gets done. Once you are comfortable accessing your inner wisdom and using appropriate dialogue in your CST session, you can start to appreciate just how varied the possibilities are when receiving this work.

In reading the case studies so far, you've also seen that people see me for a wide range of reasons and conditions. In the next chapter, I'll cover some common applications and indications for CST.

Chapter Five

Types of Conditions Craniosacral Therapy Can Help

Craniosacral therapy creates profound change with a light touch through harnessing the body's own self-corrective mechanisms. It is a very effective therapy, helpful with a wide variety of conditions from mild and temporary to life-threatening and long-standing. But when I hear someone tell me a treatment modality can cure just about anything, I'm immediately wary. If it sounds too good to be true, it probably is! Also, it's just misleading to say that a treatment will work for everyone, exclusively, without any other interventions.

I'll be honest with you: no therapy (or surgery, or medicine) works with complete certainty every time, for every person. As you're probably well aware, when someone receives a diagnosis, it doesn't mean we know the root cause of that condition. And people with the same diagnosis often present very different symptoms.

A CST session is based upon evaluation of the craniosacral rhythm, fascial restrictions, and energy holding patterns. The degree to which CST can support the relief of a particular symptom varies depending on how long the symptoms have been present, the fit between client and practitioner, and the frequency of CST treatments.

Since CST aims for the source of imbalance in a person's body rather than being driven by diagnoses or symptoms, a long list of the conditions it can treat is not very helpful. Every person, and every situation, is unique. You could say that CST treats people, not conditions.

The case studies I give in this chapter will show you some of the many different ways people have worked with CST. I've selected them to show a wide spectrum of clients, with different ages and presenting difficulties. Some had very few sessions, and some had many over the course of several years. I cover both acute and chronic conditions, and as we go along I'll explain what aspects of CST the examples highlight.

Low Back Pain

Low back pain is among the most frequent problems seen by craniosacral therapists. Here I present a couple of case studies to highlight how people can present with the same type of pain, but need to be treated in very different areas of their bodies to clear the origin of their problems.

In these two particular cases, my clients were teenagers. Generally speaking, younger clients tend to clear their body's issues in fewer sessions than adults do. I really enjoy working with teenagers, as they usually find the experience of CST to be novel and fascinating, but like to act very "cool" about it!

Case Study: Pain from Orthodontic Braces

Lucy was only 16 years old, but she'd been suffering from low back pain for nearly two years by the time she came to see me. She was able to walk only a short distance before she became very uncomfortable. Physical therapy had improved her range of motion, but hadn't alleviated her back pain. Acupuncture and massage provided only temporary relief. Lucy was feeling very frustrated, as her doctors at the pain clinic at her local children's hospital did not know what the cause or solution was. The back pain had started three months after she fell from a horse; during that time she had gone through a growth spurt and also had her orthodontic braces removed.

In our first session I noticed that she had a nice openness through her pelvis and respiratory diaphragm, but a lot of tightness in the structures that form the inside of her mouth. When I explained this to Lucy she agreed to work on that tightness in her next session, although she was very dubious that it would have any effect. She'd already seen so many different people and had no helpful results.

There had been no change in her symptoms by the next session. This time we did diaphragm releases at the pelvis, respiratory diaphragm, thoracic inlet, hyoid bone, and base of the head, but spent the bulk of the session working with her mouth and jaw. When I released tightness in her maxilla and temporal bones, Lucy felt some reduction in pain right away, but was still a little uncertain about whether CST was helping her. I explained that her body had probably had a hard time adapting to the strain the braces had put through her body, and her fall from the horse was an additional shock that it had to compensate for. Together, we were working to undo both the long-term strain and the sudden trauma.

Lucy came in for her third session feeling much better. She had been able to walk a long distance with her friends and had only a mild ache at the end. In this session I did a little work with the fascial restrictions along her midback first, then further opened up the structures in her mouth. Afterward, Lucy was pain-free, and she didn't have a recurrence of her symptoms for three years.

When Lucy's low back pain flared up while she was away at school, she came back to me for another CST session. This time we worked with her left psoas muscle, which provides postural support for the lower back, and continued opening up the structures in her mouth. By the end of the session her back pain was completely gone, and she went back to college pain-free.

Case Study: An Athlete's Pain

Mckenna was in her last year of high school, and her low back pain had been getting progressively worse over the last two years. She was so excited that she had been awarded a basketball scholarship for college, but worried about how her body was going to tolerate the increasing intensity of her training. As you would guess, Mckenna was highly motivated and worked out every day. CST's ability to align the body and help it work at its most efficient level is very beneficial for athletes, such as Mckenna; it can improve their performance and aid in the inevitable injuries they sustain.

At Mckenna's first session she described her low back pain and the chronic pain she'd felt in her left knee since sustaining a severely sprained left ankle two years before. On assessment, I found a decrease in amplitude of her CSR at her left ankle and shin, and a significant fascial restriction and energy cyst in her right hip. As we worked over the area of her right hip, Mckenna described a feeling of heat and tingling down her left leg, which she thought was very bizarre. As we continued, I noticed that her pelvic bowl widened, her hip became less compressed in the socket, and her sacrum decompressed.

By the end of the session Mckenna was standing tall, and she was amazed by how comfortable she felt. She was no longer comfortable sitting with a rounded back, and her posture was excellent and effortless, needing none of the prompting to "sit up straight" that is often called for with a teenager! She went straight to basketball training afterward and reported that she had her best shooting practice ever.

I saw Mckenna again soon after she had a bad accident in a game. She'd fallen to the ground with another girl landing on her head, causing whiplash and a mild concussion. When I examined her, Mckenna had only 75 percent range of motion in her neck, and she moved very slowly and cautiously. I placed my hands over her upper chest and neck muscles, then along the vertebrae in her neck, and Mckenna felt corresponding tingling on her neck and face and intense heat in her left ear.

We worked for two 30-minute sessions a few days apart because Mckenna wanted to make a quick recovery, and she was able to play in a game by the end of the week without any flare-up in her pain. Now, four months after working with her, she is completely free of low back pain for the first time in years.

Headaches

Headaches are another of the most common problems seen by craniosacral therapists. In the following case studies, you'll note that while the symptoms my clients presented with were similar, the causes of their headaches turned out to be very different.

Case Study: A Fall

Annabelle had recurring, debilitating headaches for most of her adult life. Medication dulled the pain but didn't help completely, and it left her feeling unpleasantly sedated. She'd seen many specialists and tried several kinds of drugs and even steroid shots into the muscles of her head and neck. All tests and scans of her brain had come back normal, and she'd pretty much resigned herself to living with chronic pain when her sister recommended CST.

At our first session, I noticed that Annabelle's CSR was diminished from her feet all the way to her ribs. Her sacrum, in particular, was barely moving at all. In contrast, the CSR in her head felt strained, with exaggerated motion. I asked if she had ever hurt her tailbone, and she replied that she hadn't.

Given my assessment, I started work at her pelvis. After completing a fascial release at the pelvic diaphragm, I stabilized the bones of her low back with one hand and gently distracted her sacrum from her last lumbar vertebra, encouraging it to move toward her feet. After several minutes, heat began to release from Annabelle's low back, and she suddenly remembered a time she had indeed fallen. Years ago, she'd been trying to skateboard during her first week of college, and the board had slipped out from under her feet. She landed on her bottom in the middle of the street, and while she'd been able to get right up and continue to ride, she was sore for weeks.

Her back was very restricted, so we worked here for quite a while. She commented how odd it was that she could be compressed in her back but feel pain only in her head. By the end of the session Annabelle was feeling giddy and relaxed, laughing about the fall. She reported only a slight reduction in her pain, but she was very interested in what she might remember next!

Annabelle's next session was a few days later, and she reported that her headache had become very intense when she left my office, and the pain lasted most of the day. She went to bed feeling discouraged, but by the next morning her headache was greatly diminished. I reassessed her and noticed that she had a robust CSR throughout her body, with minor restrictions at her tailbone, at the back of her rib cage, and at many of the bones in her cranium. We quickly and systematically worked through those restrictions, and by the end of the session her pain was completely gone. She remains pain-free to this day.

Case Study: Emotional Distress

Molly arrived at my office on a dark winter evening for her first session. She was experiencing intense headaches, along with shoulder and neck pain. She wasn't sleeping well and struggled to get through each day at work. Not long into our conversation she became very agitated, unable to hold back her tears.

I assessed her CSR and found it had a diminished vitality, which matched the persistent exhaustion she was feeling. Her rhythm was restricted through her respiratory diaphragm and throat, and there was a large energy cyst on the top right side of her head. Since she had arrived at my office in such a state of distress, I decided to guide Molly through a body scan to help her ground and reconnect with herself. I sat at her feet and held them as I talked her through feeling each individual part of her body. This calmed her sympathetic nervous system, taking her out of her strong fight-or-flight response. She was then able to feel her body on the table and be more present for the work we were doing.

I gently allowed my hands to blend and meld with the tissue above and below her respiratory diaphragm. Heat released as this area began to soften, and Molly reported feeling pressure in her head in the area of the energy cyst I'd noticed. As I moved on to her throat, the pressure continued to build and she was feeling increasingly uncomfortable, so I placed my hands on her head where she felt the pressure. She was scared and overwhelmed, and said she was unsure whether she could tolerate the sensations.

I asked Molly if she could get a sense of how much space this pressure was taking up in her head. She said, "It's in the shape of a cube and is jammed into the top of my head, squashing my brain." Her body trembled as she connected with the cube. She felt like it was threatening her life, that it had been put in her head by somebody else and did not belong to her.

This vision presented a way to access my client's inner wisdom, so I asked her if it would be okay to talk to the cube directly, without her censoring or editing what it had to say. The cube told me, "I am here to control Molly and tell her what to do." I explained that it was causing the woman a lot of pain and discomfort, which was surprising news to the cube. It eventually agreed, after a good amount of negotiation, to leave.

As Molly felt the pressure start to ease she became very agitated. She panicked about how she was going to fill this great big hole left behind by the cube. I reminded her that she now had a choice of what she wanted there. She decided to bring in a pink healing light, which she envisioned filling the hole. Molly was relieved and exhausted by the end of the session.

Molly came for two follow-up sessions and reported a reduction in the physical pain her headaches caused as well as a reduction in her emotional pain, feeling overwhelmed much less often.

Disorders of the Immune System

From the work of cellular biologist Bruce Lipton we know that the DNA is not the "brain of the cell." In other words, our bodies are not dictated solely by our DNA, but also by the environment our genes are bathed in. We can change a disease process by changing the environment we are living in—the physical environment of our cells as well as our emotional and therefore energetic environment.

In the following case study, you'll read about how using dialogue to connect with the thymus, which is a gland essential to the smooth functioning of the immune system, can create a healthy body. You will also see how changes in emotions affect cell processes.

Case Study: Asthma

Clients usually work on an issue for several sessions, but sometimes dramatic change can occur in just one visit. After this single, memorable session, Sara stopped using her inhalers, and hasn't touched them again in the last eight years. Sara is my yoga teacher and a good friend, and I feel that her practice in connecting with her inner wisdom was particularly helpful for working through an intense experience so rapidly.

Here is how she described her session:

"When my dad was diagnosed with multiple myeloma, the doctors gave him three to five years to live—Dad lasted ten! He was a walking miracle, yet every step was painful as his bones continued to atrophy.

"He had been in and out of hospitals through the years, so when he was admitted one year on his birthday, I wasn't overly worried. I should have read his symptoms a little better, because he slipped into a coma and passed away at sunset. I was very distraught that I wasn't with him when he passed, although the rest of my family was there.

"After Dad's passing I was unable to stop crying. I think it was hard on everyone else that I could not seem to stop—my aunt even had to pull me away from his coffin during his funeral—but I must have needed to cry. The crying continued back at home, too. I continued to sob uncontrollably, and while I had to stuff my emotions to teach, I often welled up in class.

"I told myself to stop. *That's enough,* I said, and then I stopped crying. But within a month I developed breathing problems and was diagnosed with asthma, which I'd never had before. The doctors prescribed inhalers and medication and left it at that. My difficulty in breathing continued, helped somewhat by the medication, but I worried about the side effects.

"I had been to one CST session with Kate before, and I loved it, so I thought I would see how this could help my breathing. I am always able to drop right in rather deeply with Kate. She is a cherished friend and gifted practitioner.

"At our session I began to tell her about my father: how sad I was that I wasn't there for him when he passed, how I had been crying for such a long time and how I made myself stop. Kate suggested that we invite my father into the session, and I felt his presence right away. He was very reassuring, saying he totally understood that I was unable to be with him when he had passed away but not to worry, he was very happy and peaceful.

"Kate then asked if we could talk to my thymus gland! I thought it was an odd request, but I trust her completely, so I said yes. She asked how my thymus was doing, and I had an immediate response: 'I can't talk; I'm drowning.' Kate described an 'energetic riverbed' from my lungs out to my arms, and we invited the dam of tears to flow through it and out of my body. It felt like I was draining the stopped-up tears from my lungs and my thymus. I realized that even though I had stopped crying on the outside, I was still crying on the inside.

"I felt immediate relief and release. I never had to use the inhalers or medication again, and my breathing returned to normal. This is nothing short of a miracle. By releasing blockages, we can all once again be free."

The "energy riverbed" that Sara describes involved my opening up her lung meridian, which is an energy pathway used in acupuncture. Interestingly, but not surprisingly, in Chinese medicine the emotion associated with the lungs is grief.

Before and After Surgery

Have CST before a scheduled surgery, whenever possible, to help the body prepare for this necessary invasion. It relieves anxiety and gives the body the opportunity to let go of unnecessary holding patterns. Clients who received CST to prepare for surgery have reported to me less scarring, faster healing, and less postoperative pain.

CST sessions after surgery usually center around the fascial changes resulting from the surgery. Fascia forms an extensive web of interconnections throughout the body, and when a cut is made across it, it will repair itself with new lines of tension that are more concerned with stability rather than with how they're going to be used. Even though the body has a remarkable capacity to adapt, this kind of tissue repair leaves us less flexible.

To work with these kinds of fascial changes, my hands connect with the tissue and follow its movement. Initially, the body will go further into its patterns of tightness, often reproducing the uncomfortable symptoms my client has been feeling. Once I have followed the tissue as far as it will go into that pattern, it will move in new directions to create a more balanced, less energy-consuming line of tension. At this point, my client and I will feel a softening and opening in the tissue.

Another effect of receiving CST after surgery is that it clears anesthesia from the body, particularly the kidneys. I experienced this firsthand when I volunteered to be a demo in one of my CST classes. My teacher put his hands under my kidneys and they suddenly felt heavy and dark. I experienced an unpleasant chemical taste in my mouth as I felt the anesthesia leaving my body from a surgery I'd had 18 months earlier. Afterward, I felt so much lighter in my body.

Case Study: Presurgery Care

In one dramatic case, I received a phone call from a client asking if his mom could have his appointment that day because she was having a lot of abdominal pain. I agreed, not knowing quite how severe the situation was. I just never know what is going to happen on any given day!

Sally looked five months pregnant when she walked across the parking lot into my office. She was unable to stand upright and was clearly in acute distress. Her abdomen had been swelling over the past few months, and the doctor told her that she had a large cyst on her right ovary. She was scheduled for her surgery on Monday, three days away, but I had no idea how she was going to make it that long.

Because she was in such distress, I approached Sally as I would a child or animal, with extra sensitivity. I felt a good amount of resistance as I moved my hand slowly toward her belly, as if there were a barrier there. I took my time, paying attention to what I felt in the palms of my hands until I felt that she was accepting my touch. I noticed her whole body start to let go a little, and her breathing softened. Within a couple of minutes of having my hand on her belly she vomited; fortunately, I was able to get my garbage can under her to make a good catch! After this she was able to relax more deeply, and she lay on her left side to ease the pain.

I carried out a dural tube "rock and glide" (which I described in Chapter Three, in Mark's case study). This had the effect of relaxing Sally's nervous system, and I helped it along by asking her to think of a place or image that was relaxing to her. She described a lake in the Swiss mountains, and we both hung out in that place for a while in our imaginations as her nervous system calmed.

My client and I then began a dialogue with her right ovary and discovered that there were unresolved issues from her first marriage and the conflict she'd felt about having more children in that marriage. When she acknowledged what she experienced during that time there was a physical letting go and a decrease in the tension in her pelvis. I finished the session by opening up the space between her occiput and first cervical vertebra, helping her regulate her nervous system by decreasing her fight-or-flight response, and inducing a still point to help her integrate all the changes.

By the end of the session, Sally was finally able to lie on her back comfortably, and when she sat up she looked very different: there was more color in her face and she was able to smile. The cyst ended up bursting on Sunday, and Sally told me that my treatment is what helped her get through the weekend. When she went in for surgery on Monday her doctors discovered that she had ovarian cancer and, because the cyst had burst, they removed all her reproductive organs along with some lymph nodes.

Sally has made a quick recovery, fortunately not needing chemotherapy. Although the cyst had grown rapidly in a short period of time, her cancer was unusual in that it was only at stage I. She has been very involved in her own care, following a specific diet to help the healing process, as well as doing extensive research on how to support her body's healing mechanisms. I gave her advice on her exercise regimen, and she had four more CST sessions with me following her surgery, mainly centered around mobilizing and freeing up the fascia in her abdomen.

Case Study: Crisis in and out of the Operating Room

Sometimes unexpected things happen in surgery, and the associated energy can have continued, unexpected effects. When Pia woke up from her brain-tumor surgery, for example, she immediately felt like something was wrong. She had gone into the hospital supported by her strong faith, feeling confident that everything would go smoothly, but now she had a new, heightened sense of anxiety. As time went on, this anxiety stayed with her.

Pia later learned that she'd had a big bleed in her brain after a blood vessel was damaged during surgery. Most of the doctors in the operating room thought that they should stop, which most likely would've resulted in death or severe brain damage for Pia. But the chief surgeon refused to abandon the surgery, and they were able to successfully stop the bleeding and remove the tumor.

I didn't know any of this when Pia came to me for a CST session. During my assessment, I felt a strong quality of holding over her heart, a paralyzed feel to the area. As my hands settled into the tissue I asked her if there was anything she knew about this part of her body. She immediately teared up and told me the story of her surgery three years before. She said that ever since, she always felt anxious.

Pia had been in a constant state of high alert, as if she were still in the surgery. When I encouraged her to feel into her heart now, she was finally able to let go of that holding around her near–death experience. With my hands and her attention over her heart, she was able to realize that she was no longer in danger and could relax. There was a softening of the tissue around her heart, and with her sense of relief came more tears. This was a profound, and very unexpected experience for Pia. It was her first experience of CST, and her sister had set up the session and informed her only 30 minutes beforehand! Pia told me that she's experienced significantly less anxiety since our session together, a result she is very happy with.

Pregnancy and Childbirth

There are so many changes that happen during pregnancy, it can be challenging for the body to keep up with it all. There are physical changes, rapid hormonal changes, and emotional changes as a woman prepares for motherhood. There's also often a spiritual opening, a wondering about where this little being (or beings) growing inside us came from. Once my twins were born, it was very obvious that they had distinct personalities and were not "blank slates"!

I had the good fortune to receive CST every week throughout my pregnancy—my friend and fellow practitioner Kathy and I would trade sessions every Tuesday morning. I had none of the complications that often occur in what was considered a high-risk pregnancy. I even started my yoga teacher–training program during this time, and I swam up until the day before my twins' birth, at 39 weeks gestation.

Despite my good health, in my last trimester I was required to have frequent nonstress tests, where they placed monitors on my belly to check the babies' heart rates. They wanted to see the heart rates going up and down as each baby responded to moving around. This procedure can induce quite a bit of anxiety with the nurses trying to find the ideal spot for the electrode and leaving you all alone in a room hooked up to a machine.

I chose to ignore the machinery and listen instead to grounding meditations by Suzanne Scurlock-Durana. I was able to bring all of my CST practice, and the knowledge I had accumulated about staying present and grounded for my work, into this situation. Through my regular CST sessions I felt very connected to the babies and knew that all was well, which significantly reduced my anxiety.

Working in Utero

A baby's first CST treatment can be held before birth; it's very special to work with a baby in utero. As I have relieved some of the structural tension in the mother, I often get a big appreciative kick or stretch from the baby as the little one moves into the new, more open space.

My friend Paola and I once worked on a woman who was a few weeks away from having her first child. The baby was breech, and the mother was trying everything she could think of to turn her around. As Paola and I worked with opening up some tight structures in the mom's pelvis and abdomen, we noticed a lot of movement from the baby. When the mother went to see her obstetrician a few days later, the baby was indeed head down, and she was able to have a vaginal birth.

Dialoguing with my babies in utero gave me some of the most amazing experiences I've had with CST. For instance, in the last two months of my pregnancy, my baby Claire changed her position from head down to breech, which meant that I would require a cesarean delivery. When I dialogued with her, she told me that she was just too squashed and had to be situated this way to be comfortable. I got the impression from Claire that it did not really matter how she came into this world; she was just excited to be born. It helped me accept the kind of birth that my children chose to have and realize just how many of my ideals I was projecting onto them.

In my CST sessions I was able to work through my sadness of not being able to birth my twins vaginally and acknowledge some of my more irrational thoughts, like feeling as if I was letting them down. This meant that at the time of their birth I was able to be as present as possible to them, although it still happened too quickly for me to take in fully. My twins were born a minute apart and only briefly brought up to me after they were born; I simply didn't have enough time to experience the complicated emotions that arose. I was able to complete that process through a CST session a couple of years later with two of my friends and colleagues in our multihands group. Then I was able to slow the whole event down and give myself time to feel the intense love and heart opening that had happened so quickly in those brief moments, safely shedding tears of joy and happiness.

Birthing

Many craniosacral therapists work with mothers during the birth process with great effect. Some even specialize in working with pregnancy and birth. They routinely help restart stalled labor, help dilation progress, and provide drug-free relaxation and pain relief.

A common form of medical pain relief during childbirth is an epidural, where doctors administer anesthesia through the dura mater, the outer membrane that surrounds the spinal cord, to anesthetize the lower half of the body. After working on many women who have had one of these, I can identify the residual effects of an epidural by the distinct feeling under my hands when I check in with the membranes. It's as if there is a little sticky feel at the injection site, and the membrane does not move as smoothly there. These women often complain of low back pain or headaches, and respond to CST treatment quickly.

I once worked on a friend of mine who'd had a particularly long, drawn-out labor and an epidural. Six weeks after her baby was born, we were visiting and I did some CST with her. We worked over the site of her epidural, and she was surprised that her legs felt much stronger when she walked down the stairs afterward.

I also worked with a woman who had vaginally birthed four children, each with the help of an epidural. After her third child she started to experience debilitating back pain and received two steroid shots in her back to help. By the time she came to see me, she had unrelenting pain in her back and right foot. In one of our sessions I worked on freeing up her dural tube by working over the injection sites. I felt a good deal of spreading and softening in the surrounding tissue and spent a long time performing a dural tube "rock and glide." Since that session she rarely feels back pain, and her foot pain is gone.

Working Through the Birth Experience

With CST, babies and children readily work through their birth experiences, and often nagging symptoms and behavior issues will clear up. The birth process, however it happens, is a time of huge change. We spend our time growing inside a womb that provides a constant temperature and pressure, and we are bathed in a fluid environment. In an ideal case, it's thought that the baby initiates the birth process, with rapid changes ensuing. It is a critical time for both mother and baby, much of it based on survival instincts.

No matter how long a mother has spent thinking and planning how the birth will go, particularly for a firstborn, she'll often experience something completely unanticipated! It is a great experience to surrender to the unknown; it's just like parenting itself. But in the heat of the moment, it's not easy to let go and stay calm.

The delicate nervous system of the baby experiences all of these new situations, so it's not surprising that most children I work with will reenact at least part of their birth process at some point. Even when things seem to have gone perfectly, the time right after birth is ideal for receiving a CST treatment, as both mother's and baby's bodies have been through a significant event. My twins were fortunate to receive their first treatment out of utero two days after being born.

One of my clients has brought her son, Alex, to me for CST since he was an infant. He was born with an irregularly shaped head, which we were able to change to a more normal shape over a few months of treatment. She then brought him back for more CST sessions when he was three years old because he was diagnosed with sleep apnea and a compromised immune system. He'd also been very hyper ever since undergoing surgery for enlarged tonsils. As I worked with Alex, it felt as though he was having a hard time eliminating the anesthesia from the surgery out of his body. Once we worked to clear it out, he started to calm down.

Then the session quickly changed focus, with Alex hanging off the end of the table upside down. I reassured his mom that all was well and to let him go with it. I supported his body as he slowly eased his way off the table. It looked and felt like a snapshot of his birth process. He really slowed it down and took his time, so I asked his mother how his birth had gone. She replied, "Very quick—too quick."

Through CST Alex was able to find a way to relive an important event in his life and rework it. Over the next couple of sessions he did a little more work around his birth, and now he seems to be all done with it. Since working through his birth experience, Alex has an easier time calming down after an upset and has been getting far fewer colds.

Babies and Children

Many childhood conditions can be helped with CST, such as torticollis (tightness or twisting of the neck on one side), nonstandard head shape, reflux, constipation, hyperactivity, ear infections, and sleep and eating problems. CST can also support children with developmental delays. As I've mentioned, Dr. John was inspired to take this work beyond the confines of the medical profession after seeing how effective CST was in helping children with autism. I've carried out CST sessions with children who have diagnoses such as sensory integration issues, spina bifida, shaken baby syndrome, rheumatoid arthritis, Down syndrome, and cerebral palsy.

Once they've experienced CST, children know when they need the work. Parents frequently say to me that their children will tell them, "I need to go and see Kate" when they haven't seen me in a while. They know that the work is helping them, even when they aren't able to express exactly how.

I worked on a six-year-old boy, Chris, who originally came to see me because he was experiencing periods of rapid heartbeat and chest discomfort. He was wearing a heart monitor so that doctors could try to identify what was happening during these episodes. His mother intuitively felt Chris's heart complications were related to the distress she experienced while she was pregnant with Chris and her own mother suddenly passed away.

The boy was very wary of my touching him, but listening to his mom read Snoopy stories helped. When I gently moved to his heart area, he became very uncomfortable and red in the face. He asked for me to lighten my touch, which I did, and tears rolled out of his eyes as he stayed with the process. It was a profound and moving experience for his mom and me as he silently worked through his difficult emotions. I worked with him a couple more times, and he has not had any symptoms since that first session.

Six months after I first met Chris, he took a bad fall playing soccer and complained of neck pain, so he asked his mom if he could come and see me. He was a lot more relaxed and chatty in this session, and I was able to relieve the compression he was holding in his lumbar spine. He frequently changed his body position as I continued to work his neck and the base of his cranium. None of this moving around interferes with the work, it just requires agility from the therapist.

As I've said before, children work quickly. Often after completing one release in their bodies, they need to get up and walk around to integrate the changes before they will accept more work. Children also often know exactly where to work, and how light the pressure should be. Frequently I have had my hand taken to the place where I need to work, or taken away and held at a distance!

Helping with Head Shape

When we are born there are large spaces between all the bones that make up the cranium to allow the cranial bones to move and adapt as the baby descends through the birth canal. Because there is so much soft tissue, the head can be misshapen after birth (plagiocephaly). This usually self-corrects within a few days, but when it doesn't, CST can be very helpful.

Plagiocephaly has become more common since the "back to sleep" campaign started in order to reduce sudden infant death syndrome (SIDS), also known as "cot death." It encourages people to put their babies to sleep on their backs rather than their sides or stomachs, and it has led to some people being too scared to put their babies on their tummies even for playtime. Combined with the use of portable car seats, babies are spending long periods of time with a curled-up spine and the backs of their heads resting on a hard surface.

Many parents of babies with plagiocephaly are told that their babies need to wear helmets to correct the shape of their heads. But during my time as a pediatric physical therapist, I saw many babies self-correct the shapes of their skulls just from being placed on their tummies to explore during playtime (note that babies should be under constant supervision while on their stomachs). CST is an effective choice of treatment if that alone is not enough.

Constipation

Constipation can be a common problem for newborn babies, especially if they needed medical interventions right after birth. CST is so effective with this problem that I became known as the "Pooping Queen" to the family of one little boy I treated! James was only four weeks old and had not had a bowel movement for three days when I first worked with him. He had inhaled meconium, which is another word for a baby's first stool. Meconium is normally stored in the intestines until after birth, but sometimes (often in response to fetal distress) it is expelled into the amniotic fluid before birth or during labor. Because James had inhaled contaminated fluid, he had required antibiotics from birth, and an adverse effect of those necessary antibiotics was that it was difficult for James to empty his bowels. James's mom is a nurse-practitioner who had received CST herself. Her medical colleagues had advised that she give him diluted prune juice or corn syrup, which didn't sound right to her, so she contacted me instead.

During my first session with James, I placed one hand on his belly and one on his back and gently connected with his tissue. I could feel the tension in his belly quickly soften and a couple of vertebrae shift in his lower spine. Within 15 minutes he had a large bowel movement and everyone was happy! I only needed to treat him one more time, a couple of weeks later, with the same results. Since then, James has had no trouble moving his bowels.

I had similar results working on my friend's baby, Riley, who made a surprise entry into the world six weeks early. I went into the neonatal unit to work on him and was immediately drawn to the base of his cranium, as it felt very tight and compressed. With babies, a working pressure is very light, often less than a gram. I had the pads of two of my fingers making the lightest of contact, and I felt a letting go and changing of alignment under my hands. I thought, *Hi there, Riley. I am so happy to be working with you today. I feel this compression here between your skull and first vertebra. Show me what needs to happen here at the base of your skull.* Then I just waited to be shown, and his body responded.

I worked on him a few more times at home to help with his constipation; each time he would have a bowel movement shortly after I left. It was interesting working with Riley, as he made his needs known to me in a direct, strong way. It was very clear energetically where to place my hands and what needed to be worked on. His body would move in such a way to let me know when we were all done working. He grimaced and cried with gusto when he was releasing something uncomfortable and visibly relaxed when an area was complete.

I shared my observation with his mom that he was particularly clear in communicating his needs; now that Riley is three years old, we are seeing that more fully! He shows no hesitation in asking for what he wants, especially when he is hungry. As much as he can protest loudly, he also has the most infectious laugh I've ever heard.

♡

In working with babies and children, once they have decided to trust a therapist they usually work very quickly. As adults, we have a lot more baggage. We have years of experiences layered over each other that reinforce our unhelpful patterns. This is one reason we have a harder time letting go and adapting to change, even when it is positive.

Dental Work

I cannot imagine a life without dentists: their work is invaluable in preventing excruciating pain. At the same time I cannot imagine how we can tolerate dental work without CST! Any visit to the dentist affects the nervous system—the roof of the mouth is intimately connected with the bones that form the floor of the brain cavity.

One client I worked with, Carrie, had required frequent dental interventions most of her adult life. She had fillings, root canals, and crowns; she also experienced a lot of jaw pain, having been diagnosed with temporomandibular joint disorder (TMD). We worked in various parts of her mouth over a number of sessions, opening up her "avenue of expression" and the structures in and around the mouth. Once, while working with an energy cyst in Carrie's gum tissue, we both noticed the distinctive taste of anesthesia. She then knew without a doubt that we were clearing the side effects of her dental work!

During another session, I was helping release an energy cyst in a tooth in her upper left jaw. As I placed a finger on either side of the molar and followed the small, wiggling, unwinding motions it made, Carrie's legs made several jerky movements. It's not uncommon to be working on a tooth and have a response in another part of the body, highlighting a relationship between the areas. Other clients have told me that they felt changes in a tooth as I worked over their hearts or bellies.

After several sessions Carrie had an improved sense of well-being, increased energy, and significantly reduced jaw pain. She continues to see me monthly as part of her self-care routine, and she always makes sure she books an appointment after any dental work!

Animals

Although I've mostly worked with dogs, all kinds of animals benefit from CST sessions—and as you'll read later, dolphins are very adept therapists!

A friend once asked me to work on her old dog, Diablo. This dog had a special place in the heart of her daughter, Mariela, who was in critical condition at the time after sustaining a head injury while fighting in Iraq. Using CST, I was able to help Diablo recover from a long-standing ear infection, but could not change the neurological damage from his hip dysplasia. However, his improved health allowed him to live long enough to see Mariela move back home, which gave them both comfort.

Another dog client, Willie, has had regular appointments with me for the last few years. CST is the only form of treatment he can tolerate because he has an intense fear of veterinarians. Any visit with the doctor is very traumatizing for everybody involved, but he will run circles around his apartment when he's told that he's coming to see me!

When Donna brought her big furry golden retriever/Labrador mix, Gator, to me, he was nearing the end of his life and she just wanted him to be as comfortable as possible. He came into my office displaying a lot of anxiety: his tongue was hanging out, he was panting, and his heart was racing. He was arthritic, having had a triple pelvic osteotomy on the right hip at five months old and a left-hip replacement when he was three years old.

Gator made himself comfortable by plonking down in the middle of the room. I worked in my usual way, feeling his CSR and locating energy cysts. I was particularly drawn to a place in his spine, at the junction of the lumbar and thoracic vertebrae. I worked on his hips and shoulders, placing my hands around them and sending in energy. Donna mentioned that she was surprised he let me touch his hips, as he was usually very sensitive in that area. By the end of our first session, Gator was a lot less anxious and quietly dozing away. His stiff hips made it a bit of a struggle to get up, but he happily walked out wagging his tail.

For the last four months of this dog's life, he happily walked in with Donna every two weeks for his 30 minutes of treatment. Then he would lie down in his favorite spot in the room and sleep while Donna got her own treatment. It became clear to my client and her husband that it was time for Gator to pass on when he began to show a lot of pain with every movement. He had a beautiful transition supported by his vet at home. I am pleased that I was able to make his last months more comfortable.

Like many of us, Donna was very close to her dogs. After the loss of her other golden retriever, Alli, Donna came in for a CST treatment with me. She later described her experience like this: "Alli died very suddenly from cancer. Since her death, I was experiencing pain and discomfort in my right hip. At the end of the session with Kate, as I was crying over the loss of Alli, I remembered that one of my nicknames for Alli was 'my right-hip girl' because that was where the breeder had clipped her to be able to tell her apart from the other puppies in her litter. This realization allowed me to release the sorrow and emotion I was holding in my body—which I'd been holding in my right hip!"

Megan's Story

With complicated diagnoses, such as cerebral palsy, CST can be used as ongoing treatment to ease chronic symptoms and also address specific issues as they occur. I'd like to end this chapter by telling you about Megan, in the hopes that you'll see just how many problems CST can help address for one person over time. Since I worked with her for a number of years, I was able to see how much could be done with just a beginner's knowledge of CST. And as my skills developed, I was able to help her even more.

Megan was very special to me. As much as I helped her and her family, she helped me in return. This is true with all my clients, as I learn and grow as a practitioner with every session. But as you'll read, Megan found a very moving and concrete way to acknowledge the work we did together.

Working CST into Physical Therapy

I met Megan when she was two years old, while I was working at the California Children's Service as a pediatric physical therapist. She was born with significant brain damage and had been given the diagnosis of cerebral palsy, and her parents were completely dedicated to doing whatever they could to better her quality of life.

Megan had big brown eyes and would give me a huge beaming smile when she saw me. Even though she could not communicate verbally, she was able to let me know through her facial expressions how she was feeling and whether something felt good or not. I helped Megan learn to move her body from side to side and develop better head control. She had limited movement and was dependent on her parents for all her needs, so I assisted in finding the right wheelchair and other positioning equipment so she could be comfortable throughout her day.

I started taking my first classes in CST as I worked with Megan and soon was able to work with her in new ways. My hands became more sensitive, so I could feel more subtle shifts and changes in Megan's body when I helped her move. I felt like I was slowing myself to her body's pace, giving her time to feel into the movements and custom-tailor them to her body. Encouraged by the results, I started to do more CST with her during her physical therapy appointments.

After one of our sessions, Megan's mom told me Megan was able to keep her head in midline for two days. This was quite remarkable, as her head was constantly turned to the right. I had not been able to change this with all the skills from my physical therapy training, yet with my beginning CST skills she responded.

Another of Megan's significant problems that we were able to address with CST was her reflux (vomiting after eating). Her food came through a feeding tube, and it was important for her basic nutrition that she be able to keep her food down, but she was vomiting three times a day. After working in 10- to 15-minute intervals of CST in this area over nine months, Megan was able to keep most of her food down and even eat some pureed food orally. While the reflux never cleared completely and her main source of nutrition continued to be through her feeding tube, it meant a lot to her parents that she had the pleasure of tasting different foods.

Continuing CST: Surgery

After I left the California Children's Service, Megan's parents continued to have her see me for CST. After she underwent major surgery for her hips, I went to the hospital immediately to work with her.

Our bones are constantly adapting and changing shape in response to the push and pull of muscles on them; this process is most active in babies and children. But children with cerebral palsy often cannot stand and walk, so their hip sockets do not fully form. Given that Megan was unable to stand without aid, she had very different stress placed on her bones than a typical child would. It resulted in the "ball" part of her hip not having a stable place in her pelvis, so the ball slowly migrated out of the shallow socket that had formed.

When I saw Megan in the hospital, she'd been placed in a hard cast (in purple, her favorite color) from her mid-chest all the way down to both feet. She seemed distressed and wasn't responding to her parents in her usual way: there was little eye contact and no smiles, and she seemed distant.

I placed my hands above and below her heart and connected with her tissue. After some time, there was a softening under my hands that continued throughout her whole body. It felt to me that Megan's body realized that she was not in danger, so it could let go. At the end of the session she looked more relaxed: her muscles were not as tense, she made eye contact, and she showed the beginnings of a smile.

Six weeks after the surgery, Megan's doctors were concerned about her progress. She wasn't forming enough new bone on her right hip to heal what had been cut. During our session together, I worked specifically on bringing osteoblasts (the cells that grow bone) to that area. I placed one hand over her right hip and the other over her sternum because the bone marrow of flat bones has a higher number of stem cells. Stem cells from our bone marrow go on to become any kind of cell we need in our bodies, and therapists can dialogue with these stem cells through CST. This holds great potential for creating change in the body.

As I monitored her CSR, I silently asked: "Stem cells, are you willing to talk to me through Megan's craniosacral rhythm?"

The CSR stopped: *Yes.*

"Can you help repair the bone tissue in the right hip?"

The CSR stopped again: *Yes.* Then I felt a buzzing sensation over her right hip, indicating the work was under way.

Ten days later, Megan had enough bone growth to be able to get out of her hip brace and make it on a trip to Hawaii with her parents. Her dad traveled there often for business, and it was one of her favorite places.

My Gift from Megan

In January 2008, at age nine and a half, Megan suddenly died. Her body shut down out of the blue, and the hospital staff was unable to stabilize her. Her memorial service was a huge gathering of people; it was incredible to see how many lives this young girl had affected.

When meditating not long after her death, I experienced the amazing sense that Megan's spirit was making a huge expansion, like a genie coming out of bottle. My feeling of her expanding has never left me. Over the years I have kept in touch with Megan's parents, who now live in Hawaii, and I continue to feel like she is still present, watching over me.

Two and a half years after Megan's passing, my husband and I were planning to attend our children's school fund-raiser gala when I noticed that one of the raffle prizes was a week in a two-bedroom condo in Maui. I had gone to the island for work in February, but wanted to be able to share the experience with my husband and children. I immediately bought my raffle ticket, took out a scrap piece of paper, and wrote down my intention that we would win and be able to enjoy this place in paradise as a family. (I even got my husband to add his signature.)

On the night of the gala a week later, my husband was in complete disbelief when our number was called out. By the time he registered that we'd won, I was halfway up to the stage! I had felt certain we'd win, even though I couldn't explain why. It became clearer to me as the night continued.

The theme for the gala was "Island Nights," so there was a very Hawaiian feel to the evening, with men in aloha shirts and women with flowers in their hair. I felt teary-eyed while watching a slideshow of all the school's children, but it wasn't until my husband leaned over and asked, "Isn't that the music they played at Megan's service?" that I really cried. At that moment, I realized it was Megan, whose presence I continued to feel, who had helped me win the trip.

Even though I no longer work with Megan's body, she has continued to teach me and keeps opening me up to new possibilities.

♡

CST can be of great support when people are reaching the end of their lives, and some craniosacral therapists even specialize in working with the dying.

I worked over a number of years with a dear woman who was being treated for ovarian cancer. I carried out my last session with her in her home about a week before she died. I helped her nervous system come to a restful place by carrying out a dural tube "rock and glide," which was about all the touch she could tolerate. It felt like I was helping her body and soul prepare for her transition.

It was a very special and surprisingly peaceful experience. In fact, I continue to feel connected to this wonderful client to this day. Like Megan, this woman's presence is often with me.

From the many cases I presented in this chapter, you can see how sometimes CST is a person's sole treatment modality, and in other cases it is used in conjunction with other modalities and interventions, in many different places and situations. Alone or in combination, CST has a lot to offer! In the next chapter, I'll talk about how you can make CST work best for you.

Chapter Six

Tailoring Craniosacral Therapy for Your Specific Needs

For craniosacral therapy to be effective, a lot depends on you as the client. You can help get your needs met by being an active participant in managing your health care: finding the right therapist for you, recognizing how frequently you need sessions, and integrating CST appropriately with the other health-care services you receive.

It's important to get clear on how involved you want to be with your health-care management and overall health. I would argue that we are each the central and most important figure in determining our own well-being. While you may have serious conditions that require expert care, at the end of the day it's you, not your practitioners, who have to live in your body and with the results of any interventions you receive. When choosing a practitioner, as a client you must be willing to be responsible and accountable for your choices, and to actively participate in your sessions.

Clear Expectations Create the Best Results

My initial evaluation form asks the question, "What is the result you would like from receiving CST?" This allows me to give my professional opinion on my clients' expectations of therapy and gives them the opportunity to get clear on their own goals. Many people come to my office just wanting to "feel better." But the most satisfying results usually stem from clients seeing a defined change in something they are passionate about.

For example, Jim, the subject of the first case study in Chapter One, had seen a decline in his golf game and was forced to limit how often he could play due to his chronic pain. The result he wanted from his CST was to be able to play as many times a week as he wanted and to improve his score. Another client came in with low back pain, and his goal for CST was to be able to go on long motorcycle rides without any discomfort. Yet another client, who is passionate about quilting, cleared her left shoulder pain and is now able to sit and quilt without any pain. When you hold a clear intention in your mind of the results you want from CST, it helps you know whether the therapy you're receiving is working. Additionally, it provides focus for each session and a guide for the overall work.

When you keep an open and clear dialogue with your practitioner, you get more value for your money! Your results will be limited if you are simply a passive recipient on the table. Pay attention to the changes that you feel in your body and in your emotions during a session; tracking these changes will be helpful for both you and your therapist.

Many people have asked me, "Has anybody else felt like this or had this response?" It doesn't matter what the situation may be—nothing a client has reported has ever been shocking to me. I think we all just want reassurance that we are not too different from everybody else!

How Frequently You Should Receive CST

By now it should come as no surprise to you that there is no single answer to how often anyone should receive CST. This may be frustrating for many people, since we like to have a clear vision of a plan before embarking on a new treatment. Generally speaking, however, the longer and more complex your issue is, the more treatment you will need.

You can work as intensively as you like with CST. When attempting to clear a difficulty as quickly as possible, you may schedule weekly or even daily sessions. Outside influences, such as work schedules or financial matters, may often dictate how frequently you can get sessions.

If you're unsure about CST in general or a therapist in particular, I recommend that you commit to having three sessions. This is usually enough time to see whether there is any progress toward the result you want. After three sessions you'll be more familiar with what CST can offer; then you and your therapist can review the progress you've made and form a plan for moving forward. For instance, you may have found some relief from your symptoms, but decide that you need more sessions or should integrate CST with another healing modality. You may have complete relief at the end of your three sessions, but find that CST supports you in other ways, such as your overall well-being, and conclude that you want ongoing sessions. You may also decide to take a break and resume treatment whenever you feel it would be helpful. Remember: you're in charge.

Finding the Right Therapist

After finding the right therapy, the next thing you'll need to do is find the right therapist! Word of mouth is the most common route to finding a good practitioner and has fueled CST's expansion over the last 30 years. Ask your friends and health-care practitioners, such as acupuncturists, chiropractors, or massage therapists, who they see. There is usually an informal network of practitioners within your local community that you can tap into.

You can also use the Upledger Institute website (**www.upledger.com**) to search for a therapist in your area. Clicking on "find a therapist" on the menu bar at the top of the home page will take you to the search function of the International Association of Healthcare Practitioners, where you can find the names and contact details of therapists in your area. (If you live in a large metropolitan or rural area and are willing to travel a bit, you can broaden your search by only putting in the first three digits of your zip code.) The site will also tell you what certifications a practitioner has, as well as what classes the person has taken, which is useful when looking for someone with specific skills. For instance, if you're looking for a therapist for your child, you will want to look for people who have taken the pediatrics classes.

Bear in mind that even practitioners who seem perfect on paper and come highly recommended may not be the best matches for you. Pay attention to your initial response and the sensations in your body when you first meet: are you relaxed or do you feel on guard? You can check in with yourself like this with anybody you meet—often, you already do. Think of times when you met someone and knew right away that you would be friends. Remember that sensation, and use it to judge how well you mesh with a particular therapist. You're not going to be friends, of course, but for the best results you need to feel trust and a positive regard from the people who will be working with you.

All good practitioners are happy to have a short phone conversation to find out if you will be a good therapeutic match. I'm often asked: "Have you worked with such and such diagnosis, and did CST help?" It's an understandable question, but as you have seen through reading this book, CST is not diagnosis-driven. Rather than asking if practitioners have treated your condition before, ask if they're comfortable working with your particular issues or symptoms.

Good questions to ask prospective therapists are, "How long have you been doing CST?" "What led you to train in CST?" and "What other healing modalities are you trained in?" Ask any questions you have, whether on practical matters or just to put you more at ease. For instance, you can ask what their hours and availability are, what they charge, and how many sessions they think you'll need. Be sure to ask whether they can accommodate special needs you may have, such as wheelchair access or mobility issues.

During initial conversations with therapists, pay attention to how you feel. Does it seem like you can ask whatever you want, or are you feeling tense or on edge as you talk? It may never be totally comfortable the first time you talk with a new person, but you can get a good sense of how you interact. Therapists will be noting how they respond to you, too, to assess if the two of you are a good therapeutic fit.

Often, you'll need to depend on your intuition when deciding upon a therapist—which is a perfectly good measure. Wayne Dyer has said that he always pays attention to his intuition when he meets somebody, and he's not afraid to follow it. He experiences a light tingling sensation in his body that lets him know when something is right—he knew right away that I could help him when he felt that tingle at our first meeting. He's also described to me the instantaneous feeling of well-being he gets during CST sessions, a felt sense he describes as "like taking a warm shower on a cold day."

Remember that you're looking for a good enough fit, not perfection; however, there are certain signs that are always helpful when evaluating a therapist. I always say to new clients that they'll know if I will be of any help to them after the first session. If you don't feel anything and sense that you're wasting your time, do not continue; it could be that this modality is just not for you.

You might also find that your condition was helped during a session, but you simply don't like the therapist's approach and style of working. We all have different preferences; you may feel more comfortable with a male or female therapist, or with an introvert or an extrovert, for example.

Therapists know they cannot be a fit for everybody and will happily give you the names of their trusted colleagues. However, the more experience therapists have, and the more CST they receive, the less this mismatch happens (which is one reason why my multihands group has been invaluable to me).

A Therapist's Background

The vast majority of practitioners come to CST through some other form of bodywork or health-care licensure such as massage therapy, chiropractic, physical therapy, and occupational therapy. It is useful to know therapists' professional backgrounds because this, along with their own personal histories, will influence how they work and what emphasis they might bring to a CST session.

One of my colleagues seamlessly incorporates her acupressure training into her sessions and says that her tai chi practice helps her stay in a fluid, comfortable place in her body as she works. I know another therapist whose years of commitment to Buddhism is evident in the great depths of stillness and compassion she brings to her practice. Another colleague credits her experience in Pilates for keeping her responsive to subtle changes in her clients' bodies. All of these practitioners are highly proficient in CST techniques, and they apply them in their distinctive styles.

♡

When clients ask me about my own background, I tell them that from the age of 18 I have been using my hands to help people with their physical bodies. The quality of my touch and the way I do it have changed since I started, but all of my experiences have helped hone the way I facilitate change in the body.

My almost 20 years of experience working in conventional health care allows me to be comfortable in many different settings. I've been in an operating theater and observed orthopedic, cardiac, and neuro surgery being performed. My work with people with many different physical and learning disabilities has helped me feel at ease with whatever symptoms a person presents with.

I am influenced by the years I spent as a volunteer teaching the Halliwick Concept. This is a way of teaching people, particularly those with disabilities, how to move safely in the water. It uses all of the amazing properties of water, such as buoyancy, to help people have incredible freedom and enjoyment when in this element. Appreciating the ways in which we can move and control our bodies in water is very similar to how I work with CST—like water, the body's mechanisms are finely balanced and can often be changed through the slightest adjustments. (You can demonstrate this to yourself the next time you're swimming: while floating on your back, roll your eyes to the right. By changing nothing but your gaze, your body will follow your focus, and you will roll right onto your tummy!)

As I have become more experienced as a therapist, I find that I've become better able to track small changes in the body and pay attention to how they affect the person as a whole. It's absorbing, delicate work with profound impact. My tracking abilities were enhanced by training with renowned therapist Peter Levine, who did groundbreaking work on how our nervous system responds to the world. He developed the Somatic Experiencing method of working with trauma, which you can read about in his book, *In an Unspoken Voice.*

Another piece of my background that influences my work is my own meditation training and practice. The discipline of quieting my mind supports me in being present during CST sessions. While I was living in Oxford, I was initiated into Transcendental Meditation and given a mantra, which I use to this day. Even though I have trained in and used many different forms of meditation since then, I still go back to that mantra in particularly difficult situations.

My yoga practice is also integral to my CST work. I took my first yoga class when I was 16, then practiced intermittently over the next few years. I always found myself seeking it out, as it brought a sense of peace and calm to my body; I had an inner knowing that it was important to my well-being. Since moving to the U.S., yoga has been a constant part of my life; I've even gone on to complete yoga teacher training.

My practice helps make my movements and positions more comfortable when I'm working on clients. I notice and let go of tension in my body more readily, ensuring that I am more perceptive with my touch. It has also taught me to become more conscious of my breath; for instance, I have a tendency to hold my breath when clients are on the cusp of a change. This leads to an increase in tension in my body, which is not at all helpful for my clients! Because of my yoga practice, I can catch myself and consciously soften my body when this happens.

And finally, an important influence in my CST work is Dr. Wayne Dyer. I first came across his work in 1999, when I saw one of his PBS shows, and I learned a lot from reading his book *There's a Spiritual Solution to Every Problem*. Now that I've worked with him, I've become well versed in his teachings, some aspect of which I incorporate into almost every session I do.

Creating Your Well-being Team

You may never have thought of it in such terms, but most of us already have a "well-being team" of people who support our physical, emotional, and spiritual needs. You probably have doctors and a dentist you see regularly (physical needs); family, friends, and colleagues (emotional needs); and an organized religion or more informal spiritual community that you participate in. Since most of us don't give this a lot of thought, our teams are often rather ad hoc! When you put time and care into building your team, you can more easily and effectively meet your needs on many levels.

When thinking about constructing your well-being team, it's important to consider what results you want from each practitioner, as well as what you want from the team as a whole. For example, take a look at the team you have to keep your car running. You need gas stations for fuel, a mechanic for maintenance and repair, a car wash for cleanliness, and so forth. Each service is important for a functioning vehicle, and it's clear that you have specific expectations of each person or business you go to for help. Now think about the team you want to support a fully functional and energetic body. My guess is that many of you would find it harder to put this team together than a team to look after your car!

The members of your team don't need to be great friends; they don't even need to know each other. All they need to be is supportive of you. You can give permission for your practitioners to communicate with each other, if you feel that would be beneficial to you, but it's also fine to keep certain things private and confide to particular people only. When I feel it would be helpful to communicate with another member of a client's team, I always ask permission in writing. I regularly communicate with clients' health-care practitioners; sometimes it's as simple as the client relaying a message between us.

A skilled craniosacral therapist will fit easily into a team with other practitioners, including medical doctors, dentists, physical therapists, homeopaths, acupuncturists, psychotherapists, and spiritual healers. Look at this team with the mind-set that you are in charge: you are setting up and coordinating a team of professionals to support you with your health and well-being goals, with varying levels of communication between the providers involved. This team will be quite fluid in its nature; you can drop modalities and practitioners at any time, then bring them back later as the need arises. You can also increase the involvement of a particular practitioner or explore a modality more deeply, if you find one that's particularly effective.

Often my clients are referred to me by a practitioner from another healing modality, and when I feel that a client would benefit from a different therapy or practitioner, I'll refer them out, too. There's a large informal network of skilled practitioners in the city I live in, and over time I've gotten to know who does what, whose work fits well with mine, and whose work suits different kinds of clients best. I prefer to receive a practitioner's work before recommending clients; but, at the very least, I'll know some of the person's patients and what results were achieved. None of the practitioners in this informal network is paid for a referral, which is sound practice both ethically and legally, to ensure that referrals are made solely for the good of our clients.

CST in Different Environments

Note that when we think of CST, we often think of a therapist in an office setting, which is how the work generally gets done. But because it's noninvasive and needs no special equipment, CST can fit into any environment; the effects of the work can even be enhanced by our surroundings.

For example, I had the very special opportunity to work in a pediatric intensive care unit with a six-year-old girl named Lina, who has rheumatoid arthritis. This experience highlighted for me that CST can work in just about any environment, no matter how challenging. The atmosphere of the intensive care unit is a stark contrast to my comfortable, relaxing office, yet we still achieved significant results.

I'd seen Lina a couple of times in my office before she was admitted into the hospital with acute respiratory distress, requiring her to be on a ventilator. When I got a phone call from her family, it was unclear whether I would be helping her heal or helping her transition into death. Her heart had stopped the day before, and the hospital staff had been struggling to keep her oxygen saturation at an adequate level ever since.

When I arrived at the hospital, I placed my hands on Lina's feet and felt her CSR. I was pleasantly surprised by the vitality of her rhythm, which gave me the impression that I was there to support her healing from this acute crisis. Based on my evaluation,

I placed my hands on the right side of her torso and started my treatment. I kept an eye on the monitor at the top of her bed that showed her blood pressure, oxygen saturation, heart rate, and central venous pressure; the staff and family were still very nervous from what had happened the day before, so there were lots of eyes watching the monitor!

After just over an hour of working with Lina we saw her blood pressure, heart rate, and central venous pressure drop and her oxygenation level improve—all good signs! Even though the little girl was heavily sedated, she would occasionally rouse and become agitated. But during and after CST she was much more relaxed when she would briefly open her eyes.

I continued to work on her daily while she was on the ventilator for the next four days, and each time we saw measurable positive changes taking place on the monitor. (It's rare for me to get so much measurable feedback during a CST session; I don't have monitors in my office!) On the first day, I noticed that it felt like her liver was struggling, and the next day Lina's mom, Denise, told me that Lina's liver enzymes were highly elevated, and she was amazed that I'd been able to pick that up before the blood tests had. But it was clear to my hands; the girl's body told me where it needed support.

The clinical nurse specialist of the unit noticed the significant, positive changes in Lina's vital signs, and as I was leaving she wanted to know what I was doing and how it worked. It was very exciting to see how the hospital staff working with Lina were so curious and receptive to what I was doing, and how seamlessly CST fit in with supporting Lina's recovery in the most intense of mainstream medical settings.

Lina made an amazing recovery, and six months later her blood test results were the best they'd been since she was diagnosed three years ago.

Multihands Sessions

As I've mentioned, in a multihands CST session you receive work from more than one craniosacral therapist at the same time. Consider using this approach when you have a complex issue or when you simply want to take care of a problem more quickly. Some people find it useful when having regular sessions is a challenge, perhaps because of a tight schedule or the need to travel long distances to reach a skilled practitioner. Personally, I like multihands work because I find that it helps me address deeply ingrained issues that I would otherwise ignore. With the support of three therapists, I am able to summon up the courage to take a look!

The customary way of working with multiple therapists is to designate one as the lead therapist, who will guide any dialogue, check in with the client during the session, monitor changes in the client's craniosacral rhythm and tissues, keep track of the time, and appropriately close the session. The other therapists support the client's body and monitor the CSR, giving the lead therapist updates on what's going on in different areas of the body. They might also jump in the dialogue with a question, but they check with the lead therapist before doing so.

Skilled therapists working in a multihands session are able to feel each other's work through the client's body, tracking tension and flow from their own hands to the areas where other therapists are working. For instance, the therapist at the head would feel when a release was occurring under the hands of the therapist at the right foot. This provides deep, comprehensive healing support for clients.

My colleague Robyn and I offer multihands sessions to our clients once a month. Usually these clients have been receiving regular CST with one of us, but find this extra "boost" to be very helpful. Two sets of skilled hands can address more issues and work more deeply and efficiently.

One client who'd been receiving regular bodywork for years and then had a multihands session with Robyn and me for the first time had this to say: "The session was amazing. I really didn't know what to expect, yet I never expected what I got! I'll start by telling you the tangibles: my right shoulder is now level with my left. I feel very 'square' and aligned, and I'm pain-free. During the session I felt amazing sensations—it seemed that all my trouble spots were lighting up sequentially. I could imagine what you were doing, or intending to do, and it all felt very natural and organic, as though it was all supposed to happen for good reason. I felt like a noodle afterward and throughout the day—in a good way!"

Case Study: Multihands Session with Wayne Dyer

While attending a conference in Florida, I learned that Wayne was staying with family close by. His back was in pain, so I arranged to do a multihands session with him before I flew home. I was with two of my cherished friends and colleagues, Kathy and Robyn. We've worked together frequently with other clients, and it was a treat to do so again.

As with every multihands session, we carried out an evaluation of Wayne's CSR and decided where each of us was going to work. Robyn was at Wayne's left foot, Kathy was at his sacrum, and I was on the right side of his respiratory diaphragm. Once we had all settled into the session, we checked whether the three of us could connect with each other energetically, and noted a line of tension that connected the three of us from his left toes up through the sacrum and over to the right side of his diaphragm.

Wayne became more aware of discomfort in his left thigh, and I asked him if it was related to a tennis injury we'd been working with before. He said no, but he could now clearly remember another accident he had on a tennis court, when he ran full force into the post for changing the height of the net. He hit his left thigh so hard that he felt he might lose function in his leg altogether if he didn't keep moving. He walked around and around the court for over an hour before he felt he could leave, and there was a massive amount of swelling and bruising afterward. We could still see a slight indentation in the muscle of his left thigh, even though the accident happened more than 30 years ago.

As we worked, his CSR was off and his thoughts kept returning to that time, which confirmed that his body was working on the impact of that event. He then connected the feeling of walking around that tennis court with a personal frustration he was currently experiencing (it's very common to have an old injury surface in a session that highlights a current life issue).

Robyn followed the unwinding of tissue in Wayne's left leg as his respiratory diaphragm and sacrum softened under my hands and Kathy's. The discomfort in his left thigh started to ease. By the end of the session he felt the pain in his left thigh and the chronic tension in his low back had lessened significantly. As always, he also felt deep relaxation and an increased sense of well-being.

If I'd been the only therapist in the room that day, I would not have been able to provide all the support Wayne needed for such a complete release of that long-standing pattern. Alone, I might've made some progress toward it; but with three therapists, it all was released in the space of an hour.

Comprehensive Therapy Programs

A *comprehensive therapy program* treats several clients at a time over five days and is offered through the Upledger Institute (although I've also seen groups of craniosacral therapists get together and offer a similar format). Participants receive multi-hands CST every day—sometimes twice a day—along with other healing modalities, depending on the needs of the clients and the skills of the therapists involved. You might have lymph drainage, visceral manipulation, acupuncture, massage, sensory integration, and other treatments incorporated into a single day.

My friend and colleague Sarah has participated in and run a number of these programs. Her description, which follows, will help you appreciate the less tangible aspect of the work:

"The collective process of each group of people at a five-day program generates a shape, or common journey. As each individual shares the story of their sessions with the group every morning, the group's nature changes. It takes the feeling of 'I am not alone in my suffering' to a profound level, into, 'I am sharing this healing; we are healing together.' Ultimately, it emerges as 'There is healing potential everywhere.' In some way, these five-day programs create their own environment as well, and you never quite know what the nature and tenor of that environment might be, except that there is deep trust in the process."

She told me, "As you keenly know, in order to do multihands work therapists have to let go of their own agendas and let go of their ego orientation. When there is a large-scale letting go into the whole of a comprehensive program, the 'whole' begins to work therapeutically on everyone. Because of the daily rotation of therapy teams, each client has the opportunity to work with many or all of the therapists—for a 10-client program, there can be as many as 36 therapists.

"For several years I did not have words to describe the changes that I felt happen. I still feel that words don't really touch the reality, the heart altering, the profound expression of what humans can do when they put their minds to a task. I just know that I have been changed internally by having let go, and by having been part of the whole of this community."

Working with Dolphins

When I was studying at the Upledger Institute, Dr. John recounted stories of how he included dolphins into CST teams for clients. He began working with captive but free-swimming dolphins in the mid '80s. He'd have three or four therapists working with a client in the water. The dolphins would swim around them and use their rostrums (snouts) to touch the therapists in places that the therapist needed help before working directly on the client. Everyone clearly felt that the dolphins were instructing the therapists.

Now there's a yearly comprehensive therapy program in the Bahamas that uses CST in the water with dolphins, who participate in sessions at their will. The clients who attend have usually already been receiving CST for some time, and the array of conditions that has been helped include cerebral palsy, autism, closed head injuries, PTSD, spinal cord injuries, and autoimmune disorders.

Recently, I was left in tears by footage of such CST work with dolphins. I watched dolphins, of their own volition, touching a young boy with cerebral palsy. Afterward, this boy's body was relaxed enough to be cradled by his mother for the first time. A short, powerful DVD was created and presented at the conference by the boy's mother, who after that first trip to the Bahamas was inspired to become an advanced practitioner in CST.

Another interesting story I heard from Dr. John was about the time he was giving a talk in Edinburgh. It was attended by the head of the physical therapy school I had gone to, and Dr. John mentioned that she was very skeptical of the work. As he demonstrated CST on students, he would sometimes ask out loud for some dolphin energy whenever he felt that a bit more energy was needed.

The head of the physical therapy school noticed that every time he called on the dolphins, her hearing aid buzzed and crackled. A month or so after Dr. John got back home to Florida, he received a package from her containing her hearing aid with a note saying that she hasn't needed it ever since his demonstration. She suggested that he ought to investigate the hearing aid to find out what had happened!

My own felt sense of how much dolphins can support this work was bolstered by my experience of swimming with wild dolphins. On two occasions while swimming in the ocean off Maui I have been completely surrounded by 30 or more of these beautiful creatures. As I swam with them I got the sense that they were checking me out, and that somehow they were able to read me energetically, like the way I read my clients when I am working but much deeper and more completely. I also felt that my brain was rewiring, changing in response to all the clicking and different vibrations they create in the water. The sensation was similar, but more enhanced and nuanced, to how it feels when I have received work on my brain in CST sessions.

Case Study: Combining It All for the Best Results

This case study demonstrates how all the information in this chapter fits together: you can gain powerful results, even when the challenges are multiple and complex, when you find the right therapists and treatment modalities, have the right frequency of sessions, and enhance traditional medical interventions with multihands therapy and comprehensive therapy programs.

Over a period of four years, a group of colleagues and I worked with a young soldier, Mariela, who sustained a severe head injury and multiple injuries to her body. She was in the Army, and had completed one tour in Iraq with her husband three months after their daughter had been born. She was on her second tour in December 2004 and had just made the grade of sergeant when she was critically injured. She was in a coma for more than six months, and after almost two years of hospitalization on the East Coast, with multiple surgeries and other traumatic medical procedures, she was transferred to a Veterans Administration (VA) hospital near her hometown of Livermore, California.

I was part of a team of craniosacral therapists that began providing CST to Mariela after she was transferred back to California in August 2006. For someone with such a high level of trauma, it was best for Mariela to receive multihands work from experienced therapists, so we set up a weekly rotation enabling at least two advanced craniosacral therapists to work with her while she was in her hospital bed. At times, five therapists treated her at once.

When we began, Mariela was talking with a stutter, had significant memory loss, and required full assistance to get in and out of bed. She was very scared of being moved, as it caused her great pain, and the medical staff had to move her often during the day. Yet within a short period of time, Mariela began to remember our names, and looked forward to her sessions. Her memory improved, her speech began to clear, and she became more motivated to transfer herself out of bed.

During the first couple of years we worked together, Mariela's chief complaint was intense pain in her tailbone and pelvis. Her right arm was also painful and severely limited in its range of motion in the shoulder, elbow, wrist, and fingers. Yet after her second CST session she spontaneously used her right arm to eat her lunch.

Many of our sessions revolved around releasing the fascia where her breathing and feeding tubes had been. Both of these interventions were lifesaving for Mariela, but they also had a profoundly painful impact on her, making it difficult to heal. The feeding-tube site, in particular, has been a place that has consistently been worked on. Six years after the removal of the tube, the site is finally not leaking.

In 2007, with Mariela using a wheelchair and just beginning to take steps on her own, we started working in a hydrotherapy pool. At the end of her first session she was very relaxed and said that she felt like she had slept for two years, so we decided that the pool was the optimal place for her treatments to take place. The water has provided great freedom of movement, and Mariela now often spontaneously rolls over 360 degrees, when before rolling caused her a lot of anxiety and pain. She is able to work on her walking and postural alignment directly after the sessions, feeling into the changes that have occurred and helping integrate the newfound freedom in her body.

Mariela continues to surprise her VA medical team with her progress. When she was first injured they thought that she would not come out of her coma; later they predicted that she would require round-the-clock nursing care. It's unusual for them to see someone continuing to improve six years after a traumatic head injury, but it's clear to all who've known her that she continues to make progress in all aspects of her being. Now she's able to walk short distances with a quad cane and transfer in and out of bed independently, as well as swim 25 laps, get in and out of the pool by herself, paint amazing pictures, ride a horse and buggy, and play the piano. She's even learning to salsa dance.

In addition to her medical team at the VA, Mariela and her family have set up a team to provide her with an intensive program of CST, yoga, chiropractic work, therapeutic horseback riding, acupuncture, and Vasper (a low-impact exercise routine). This integrative team communicates through Mariela's mother, who acts as team leader.

CST has been the most consistent part of Mariela's healing and recovery for several years in a row. She's making amazing progress primarily through her own determination and because her parents made it their mission to support her in getting all the therapy she requires to succeed. She's been able to identify and live from, as she described it, "a place of confidence in myself." Mariela is clear and determined that she will continue to improve.

Now that you know how to find a craniosacral therapist and create your own well-being team, let's take a closer look at how you can be sure to get the most benefit from your CST sessions.

Chapter Seven

Enhancing Your Craniosacral Therapy Experience

In this chapter you'll learn about practices that will help prepare you for your CST work and continue to support you in your everyday life. I'll give you practical ideas about how to get more out of every session while you're on the table, as well as how to extend the effects. At the end of the chapter I'll describe a series of short sessions I did with people who had limited time but lots of motivation to take care of themselves, to highlight how to get the most out of your work. All the suggestions and examples are given to spark your imagination—there are endless ways to enhance what you experience with CST.

How Does CST Fit in for You?

Craniosacral therapy is considered "complementary" health care, but don't get that confused with "complimentary"—it's certainly not free! It's not usually covered by medical insurance, so deciding to have CST means that you're committing not only your time, but your money as well. Many of my clients have medical insurance and use CST to address what their insurance-covered providers cannot. Others do not have insurance at all—a number of my clients who fall into this category use CST as part of their preventive care. Still others have only emergency insurance coverage, as they don't use conventional health care for any other reason, and use CST for everything else.

People try CST for many reasons. Some have tried to address their problems with medication and surgery, but find that neither provides relief, so they come to CST as a last resort. Others have had success with allopathic medicine, but recognize they have needs that conventional treatments can't address. Even when a medical intervention like surgery is the answer to a problem, there are additional physical, emotional, and spiritual issues that will inevitably come up during that time, and it's not within the role of the surgeon to tend to them all. Healing is multifaceted, and that's why we all need a team to help us.

Why are *you* coming to CST? Knowing your reasons will help you get the most benefit from your sessions.

Over the years I've noticed that certain people are able to work rapidly and deeply in a session, even if it's their first time and they know very little about CST. Some of these individuals have a regular meditation or spiritual practice; others do yoga or tai chi; and still others are experienced in a healing modality such as massage or talk therapy, and may have used them to work through a significant event in their life. All have something in common: they maintain a practice or have had an experience that helps them access their own inner wisdom. They know how to be centered and grounded, even if they wouldn't necessarily use those words.

These people are familiar with their unique learning and healing process; they know it's not linear, and that there will likely be unexpected discoveries. Having a practice that centers and grounds us lessens our fear and resistance to exploring uncomfortable sensations and feelings. I see speed, depth, and specificity in my work with clients who are deeply aware and in touch with themselves. These sessions are very efficient, like in the case study of Sara, who cleared her asthma in one session.

CST works at the very center of our being, and we can access that core place in numerous ways. It's important to feel at ease in your session, so you can work in whatever way that suits you best. I know some people who want to discuss every sensation they experience, while others track the changes in their bodies quietly. Some clients talk all the way through the session; even when the talking is not relevant to what's happening in their bodies, there is a continuing positive change in the tissues, so I know that their talking isn't inhibiting their sessions. No matter how much you choose to talk, if the work becomes overwhelming or too intense, be sure to tell your therapist; the session can be adjusted to your comfort level and pace.

There is a palpable, sacred feel in the room when important and significant change is occurring. Those who have observed me working have said that just being in the room had a positive effect and imparted a sense of peacefulness in their bodies. Whenever people have accidently walked into a CST session, they've known instinctively that they need to be quiet and respectful. That said, if you were to witness a session you just might find us laughing. Humor is a great way to process, and laughter can be as powerful as tears in processing emotional holdings. The insights and "aha" moments that people share are gifts to me; I get to experience wisdom, in its many forms, on a daily basis.

Set Aside Time to Integrate the Work

To enhance your CST sessions, it is important to set your session time as something that's just for you. You don't want to be answering a text or phone call during your time on the table! I've had people rush late into my office, asking to cut the session short so they can get to a meeting. Although I'm happy to accommodate a tight schedule, I feel that if you do this, you are definitely short-changing yourself.

Leave yourself a little time after your session to ground and reorient yourself before popping right back into your busy life, and use grounding practices to help you deepen and extend the changes that have occurred. I've watched some people walk out my office door and go right back into their old holding patterns . . . I want you to keep your gains! So if you don't have any practices established yet, the rest of this chapter offers some ideas on where to start.

If you're a kinesthetic learner, moving your body through yoga, tai chi, dance, or another method can be very helpful for extending the effects of CST work. Some people love to write or draw in journals after a session. You can also gain deep insights by taking note of your dreams, passing thoughts, and emotions immediately before or after a session. If a new memory surfaces, you may want to verify the information with family or friends, like Jim did in Chapter One; he remembered that he had hip problems as a baby, and a phone call to his aunt confirmed that he'd indeed been in a hip brace.

Whatever your predisposition, you'll get more out of every session when you set some time aside to process what the session has brought up for you. Reading inspiring books or listening to uplifting CDs can be useful, and I have a little library that I routinely lend out to clients when topics are relevant to their session (my selection, of course, includes many Wayne Dyer CDs). One book that is a great resource is *The Art of Extreme Self-Care* by Cheryl Richardson, which has many practical suggestions on ways to care for yourself. I also have a CD I recorded at the request of some of my clients, which helps people relax and get to know their body sensations in a deeper way. It includes a short meditation for children who have nightmares and difficulty getting to sleep.

Sometimes you may leave a session having received very specific "orders" from your inner wisdom, with actions to take that will create the change you desire. For example, when I was in Vancouver, I met up with Nicollette and her family for the first time since we'd worked together in Maui. Nicollette's sister, Ashley, was experiencing intense back pain that radiated down her left leg and created a feeling of pins and needles in her left foot, so we decided to do a CST session together.

When I was working over Ashley's heart area, we invited her heart into the session to tell us how it was feeling. It expressed how tired it was, and that it felt like Ashley made no time to listen to it because she was too busy working and going to college to pay any attention.

We then invited Ashley's inner wisdom to support her in figuring out her next steps. It showed up as a bright white light in her mind's eye, and Ashley gained the understanding that she had the choice to either make time to check in with her heart or continue to have the pins and needles slow her down.

Ashley agreed to make time to check in on a daily basis. But when we asked her heart if that sounded like a good plan, it replied, "I don't believe her!" Ashley was a little shocked by this response. She knew that this was an important commitment she was making to herself, and she assured her heart that this time she would follow through.

Ashley has kept her promise and has steadily felt improvements. The pins-and-needles sensation is disappearing, and she feels much less stress and fatigue on a daily basis.

This dialogue between Ashley and her heart demonstrates how essential it is to listen and follow through with insights we gain in our sessions if we want to reap the full potential of the work. We are not passive recipients when we are on the table, and we continue to have a responsibility to ourselves when the session's over.

Specific Practices That Can Enhance CST

Now let's take a look at some things that can be used during your session, to enhance the work; after your session, to help you maintain and deepen your gains; and in your everyday life, to center and ground you.

Breath Awareness

Throughout CST sessions I'll observe my clients' breathing patterns, which gives me an indication of how relaxed they are (or not!). I also pay attention to my own breath to ensure that I'm staying relaxed and present. It's common to take in a big breath and sigh during sessions; these breaths often coincide with the tissues' letting go of a holding pattern. So let them happen as you feel them arise.

Sometimes, breath has a story all its own. For example, I had a client who started taking shallow, rapid breaths midway through a session. When I checked in with her to make sure she wasn't feeling overwhelmed, she said that she was familiar with this breathing pattern. It seems that when she got anxious, her breathing changed, she'd feel really warm, and then she'd usually burst into tears and spiral into a feeling of overwhelm; she was surprised that she was breathing this way now, though, since she felt relaxed on the table. I encouraged her to stay with those short breaths, as I could feel the heat her body was creating help her tissues start to open and relax. It was fascinating to us both that her body chose that breathing pattern to give her tissues the activation they needed to let go of their holding.

There are times when you might experience discomfort as your therapist works on an area that is tightly held. One common place is the base of the cranium where it meets the neck, since we have a thick layer of muscle there that's often tight, protecting that vulnerable spot. The technique used to open it often gives a feeling people describe as "intense" or "a good pain." When this happens, I encourage clients to pay particular attention to their exhales, inviting their bodies to let go of whatever tension they no longer need.

Some clients feel that it's suddenly easier to breathe during their sessions, particularly through their diaphragms. They can feel the air moving through their bodies from the inside. This can be a really exciting new sensation! I encourage them to take careful note of this change and then spend some time at home afterward observing their breathing, paying attention to the feeling of their breath moving.

Breath-awareness practices, such as *pranayama* in yoga, are also useful both on the table and after. I've personally found it useful in my own sessions!

Movement

I often feel the need to move when I receive CST, and I follow that impulse, knowing that my therapist will support me as I do. Following a movement is one way I access my inner wisdom; it helps me deepen my understanding of what I'm processing, and shows me how to let it go. I encourage you to allow your body to move as it wants to. You may never feel an impulse to move, or you may be like me, at the far end of the spectrum in terms of being a kinesthetic person—most of my own sessions involve some kind of movement on the table. You'll find your own way to move (or not), to make your sessions most effective.

Moving during CST can make you feel vulnerable, but I encourage you to follow the impulse if it arises and you feel safe. You are in control, and you always have the choice to stop! On a practical note, remember that the tables are narrow; if you find yourself feeling that you are precariously close to the edge, you can simply move back to a safe place in the middle of the table and you will drop back into your session again.

Moving is a good way of continuing your process after a session, as well. A practice called *Continuum Movement,* founded by Emilie Conrad, is very helpful in enhancing your ability to find and follow your body's impulses. Continuum Movement explores how bodies move when there are no demands placed on them. You use breath and sounds to vibrate through tissue and loosen restrictions, or "soften the inhibitors." Then the body can move as it wants, rather than having to move to perform a task. Moving in new ways that aren't our habitual patterns can create profound change.

I've always been able to release whatever's going on for me most easily in water. I've experienced some incredible CST sessions in it, but I've also had fantastic releases doing my regular workout in the pool or just simply moving and playing in water. On land, yoga is one good method for processing after CST work, especially as a home practice. That way, you can choose poses that feel right and stay in them as long as you want. After a session, when I go into my quiet time at home, I'll continue to follow any spontaneous impulses I have to move and see where they take me, paying attention so I notice when things feel complete.

During my sessions with clients who practice yoga, when we feel areas of the body opening up, we will discuss the yoga poses that address those same muscle groups. For example, if we feel the hip adductors (the muscles on the inside of the thigh) open, we may discuss a "seated forward fold." I ask them to pay attention to their yoga practice afterward, and they commonly describe to me later how much more deeply they can go into poses. One client said, "I could not believe the difference in my adductors in my next yoga class. I felt no holding or tightness, when before I always felt like they might snap in a seated forward fold." In the quiet time after a CST session, the yoga pose called *viparita karani* is very helpful to most people. In this position, you simply lie on your back with your legs resting up on the wall in front of you.

I encourage you to find a movement practice that supports your well-being. Practices such as tai chi and Pilates are great ways to continue opening up and stabilizing the changes that happen in a CST session. Simply taking a relaxing walk after a session can also be a great way to integrate the work. There may be some open space nearby where you can hike or sit in the peace and quiet of the outdoors. You can take a nice stroll around your neighborhood or simply move slowly through your backyard.

Sound

Similar to the feeling of wanting to move your body, you may have the impulse to make a sound at some point during your CST session. It can take courage to do so, especially in front of your therapist! Just know that your therapist will support you in whatever you choose to do. I'll often make these sounds along with my clients, to help alleviate any embarrassment they might feel.

One sound I've found to be helpful is one that sounds like "ohm" or "voom," but any sound that comes to you is fine. Sounds create a vibration you can feel in your body, creating openness and helping bring a sense of calm. They're particularly useful when you're feeling overwhelmed.

Words may come to you that you'll feel the need to say out loud. This can happen when working anywhere in the body, but I've noticed it most often when opening tissues in the throat and mouth. Sometimes a song may spontaneously come into your head, and it'll feel good to sing it or have it sung to you. While not all therapists can carry a tune (one of those therapists being me), we're usually pretty game to try! I've even participated in multi-hands work where we all sang to our client upon request.

I usually have quiet, unobtrusive music playing in my office. You may consider bringing in your own music to therapy as well. One of my clients gave me a CD that plays a mantra from her particular spiritual practice, which I play during her sessions.

Even if you don't use sound during your session, you may find it helpful afterward. Whether you use nonsense sounds or whole words, loudly or softly, the privacy of the car is a good place to make noise! I've found singing along to kirtan CDs (a call-and-response form of singing) particularly helpful after a mouth-work session.

One client told me that after a session in which we had focused on opening her neck and throat, she noticed much greater ease in her body at choir practice the following week. She felt the newfound opening in her throat brought even more enjoyment to her singing, and she was able to maintain this spaciousness through her regular rehearsals.

Imagery

A scene or picture often comes to clients during their sessions, one that helps them understand what they're working with. If an image appears for you, it can be helpful to regularly check in with it afterward. As an example, consider a client of mine who had intense bladder pain. When I asked her if there was anything we could bring into her bladder that would help with its healing process—a color, temperature, or any other quality—she said, "A cool blue gel." We visualized bringing this into her body, and she had no pain in her bladder or urethra at the end of the session. Now, as part of her daily practice, she continues to envision this gel, usually as she lies in bed at night before going to sleep.

This method of using our imagination is a way of accessing our inner wisdom. The first few times can feel awkward, and you may feel some self-doubt. But there is valuable information to be gained from engaging with your unique inner imagery.

A good friend shared with me some of what she saw in one of her most memorable and powerful sessions: "I saw the image of a huge keychain, with hundreds of keys—I realized that I was trying to find the right key for every situation, to make myself 'fit.' I then met one of my guides, who taught me to dance; subsequently, the keys transformed into a tambourine, which I danced with, feeling a sense of fitting in just as I am, and celebrating that. Now whenever I see that keychain in my mind's eye, I realize I'm trying to fit in or fix a situation, and I'm reminded that I simply need to be myself."

Dreams

Dreams can be seen as a way to access your nonconscious mind, and many believe that you can find meaning and solutions in them. Clients often report that symptoms and symptom-related dreams show up just before a session, as if the body is highlighting what needs to be worked on.

I have no training in interpreting dreams, but many times I've had people describe theirs to me during a session. Fortunately, I haven't needed to offer an analysis, as they've been able to find their own answers as the session unfolds.

During one such session, a client came in and described to me the dream she'd had the night before, in which a tigress had appeared. We began the session at her right pelvis, and she asked what color the chakra was in that area. When I told her it was orange, she said, "This is what the tigress was showing me. It's where I have fear. When I was terrified of opening up my own company 20 years ago, I had my right ovary removed; and now I'm afraid to take my next career step. The tigress is a sign for me to have courage."

The information was streaming out of her. As she talked, I noticed her right sacroiliac joint opening. There was a new sense of space in her pelvis, and I invited her to feel into that sensation. She left with a renewed sense of purpose, willing to take the next step in her career.

It's common to have deep, restorative sleep after CST, and to have interesting dreams. Write down any images you remember when you wake up. I've found it useful to go back and reread what I wrote a few weeks later; they always make a lot more sense to me than when I wrote them down, though I can't say why.

Archetypes

In their sessions many people find there are underlying themes that are also reflected in fairy tales and myths. Although the specifics of our situations may differ, all of us are often working on the same core issues! I listen to fairy tales with my children in the car, and I'm surprised by how much insight I continue to gain about my own life every time I listen to them.

You may gain insight from reading or listening to stories, too. One author I frequently recommend is Clarissa Pinkola Estés. Listening to her CDs can help you gain further insight into your CST sessions.

You may also find connections to your own life issues through reading Joseph Campbell's work on mythology, which includes many wonderful traditional stories and imagery from around the world.

Journaling

Some people love to write. But even if you don't think of yourself as a writer, journaling can be helpful. Remember that it's just for you, not for anyone else to read, and it's a great way to express your thoughts, dreams, and emotions.

Journaling was not something that I was drawn to growing up, but I have learned to enjoy it and have found it very beneficial. You can write down descriptions of your CST sessions, and often as you write, your understanding of your experience deepens. If you've done a lot of intense emotional work, your journal is a safe place to put it; you can read through it again when the emotions are not as raw and you can absorb more information. Some of my clients who journal regularly will access information during CST work that they later explore further with a talk therapist. Some people bring in their journal when they see me, because they like to write down information and impressions as soon as possible, before they forget.

You can also use writing to help formulate your intentions when you prepare for your CST sessions. The scope of your questions can be cast wide. Questions to consider include: *What results would I like? Is there an area in my body that needs relief? What pattern of pain can I gain more insight into? Is there a reason my pain shows up at a particular time or place? Is this issue connected to a past event?*

I always encourage people to take some quiet time with themselves after a session, to check in and notice any new sensations. This is a great time to write down your experience, what you noticed, and any interesting thoughts that arose during the session. Your body is still actively working on a session for at least 24 hours afterward, so this reflective time is a way to capitalize on the process. You may find that writing helps your body to continue softening and releasing. It's not uncommon to experience new emotions and sensations as you write.

Drawing

If you're more inclined to draw than write, you can use that medium to help continue your process after CST. A clear image may come to you during your session, compelling you to draw it. Some clients see amazingly vivid colors during their sessions, and drawing or painting these colors is a way of continuing their process. Give yourself permission to follow your impulses.

Once, after seeing a compelling image in a session, the impulse to draw came to me. I had to go out and buy a bunch of art supplies, because it's something I never do! Interestingly, I knew exactly what kind of oil pastels and paper I wanted. Drawing was an incredibly powerful process for me, and one that took me by surprise. It gave me a sense of being in charge of how I dealt with a childhood experience, when at the time it happened I had no power. I even surprised myself with my artistic talents and the fact that I was able to successfully convey my imagery.

Spiritual Practices

Although CST is a physical, "in the tissues" technique, it inevitably impacts our emotional and spiritual selves. How much the spiritual aspect of CST is brought to the forefront in a session depends on both the client's and practitioner's comfort. If there's a mismatch between the perspectives of you and your therapist, move on and find the right fit.

For some people, their spiritual practice is an integral part of their life and necessarily forms a major part of their processing in a CST session. I'm open to all belief systems, as I feel that they all share the same essence and truths. I feel the peace and support when my clients access their spiritual guidance, however it shows up; it's a beautiful and sacred thing to feel. One client I work with has a strong connection with her Christian church, for instance, and when we're working on emotional issues she effectively calls upon the Holy Spirit to come support her during the session.

When my clients tap into their spiritual beliefs, it usually helps them stay with sensations or emotions that could otherwise feel too intense. People with a meditation practice they've used for many years will often employ mindfulness techniques during and after their sessions. In addition, it can be very beneficial to simply spend quiet time scanning your body after your session.

A dear friend of mine described how she saw this connection between CST and spirituality: "As a spiritual seeker I believe it is my responsibility to take care of the outer temple that houses my soul. With this belief in mind I tried CST, not knowing what to expect. I quickly learned that physical pain is a manifestation of much more, and CST provides the opportunity to identify and heal emotional pain through the body. There is an intricate dance between our outer and inner selves, and we can choose to either lead or follow.

"I did my usual spiritual practice of contemplation on the morning of my first CST session, asking for healing guidance. As I lay on the table, the physical touch of the practice allowed my body to relax and respond on its own. I discovered areas of pain were really emotional 'hot spots,' holding negative memories and feelings. We talked about these issues at times, and other times I sang my mantra to myself, as my body released and shifted. I left that first session feeling energized and excited about this healing modality.

"CST has become an integral part of my lifelong spiritual quest. I never imagined how it would enhance my awareness. During my sessions I see colors, memories, symbols, and future possibilities. Participating in this dance is not always easy, but it's always rewarding. I was told I would never be able to run again, and I just completed a half marathon. Imagine the possibilities!"

♡

Many years ago, I was introduced to an Indian guru named Mata Amritanandamayi, or "Amma," which means "mother." Amma is affectionately known as the "hugging saint." She has hugged millions of people around the world and comes to the Bay Area twice a year. She honors all religions, and people from a wide variety of backgrounds regularly go to see her.

The first time I received *darshan* from her (which is what her followers call receiving a hug), it was an amazing experience. She was greeting thousands of people that day, yet when she made eye contact with me it was the most present and nonjudgmental connection I had ever felt. That experience was an inspiration to me: I got to know and feel how important it was to keep taking steps to be more present and less distracted in my work with others. It gave me a gold standard that I can keep working toward.

Connecting to Special Places

You may find yourself in a special environment that offers support and provides unique ways of enhancing your experience. Recall that when I worked with Nicollette in Maui, I invited her to become aware of ocean sounds to support her. You might find yourself in a similar yet unusual situation when receiving a CST session—perhaps in the Bahamas with dolphins! You might also energetically connect with a place that's special and supportive for you, such as the woods or a particular mountain.

I worked in some places of spiritual significance when I had the amazing opportunity of joining the "Experiencing the

Miraculous" tour led by Wayne Dyer in June 2011. I was part of a 160-person group visiting three special sites: Assisi, Italy, where St. Francis lived; Lourdes, France, where St. Bernadette had 18 visions of the Blessed Lady; and Medjugorje, Bosnia, where the Blessed Virgin Mary has been appearing since 1981.

Everybody who was attending the trip was a follower of Wayne's work, and open to new experiences. This was a unique setting, where we could find many ways to enhance personal changes we experienced. The trip provided ample opportunities for spiritual connection and exploration. We had time for reflection; visits to inspiring landscapes; and the company of supportive, like-minded people.

In Assisi, special permission had been granted for Wayne to give a talk in the sacred space of the Abbey San Pietro, and I was invited up to the microphone to share my experience of working with Nicollette. After the talk ended, I was in high demand! During the rest of the trip I worked with 23 people in very focused 30-minute sessions (usually I do 60-minute sessions).

It was an intense and amazing experience working this way. People experienced many changes in that short amount of time, and I believe it was due in large part to their expectation that something amazing could happen for them, and their belief that they could access their innate ability to change and heal. More important, after their sessions ended, they were still immersed in the group energy of possibility, and in locations that held special meaning. For example, in Lourdes it was possible after a CST treatment to bathe in holy water—that's not the kind of thing you can usually do after CST!

Here are a couple of examples of what people experienced with CST on this trip, and what happened for them afterward:

Sandy had her very first experience of CST on the trip. She had chronic neck pain for many years and had started breaking out in giant hives in the past six months. She had medication, but she took it only when the hives were making her miserable.

During her session, Sandy was able to quickly and easily relax and feel changes taking place in her body. I worked over the right side of her pelvis and at her neck, which included opening up the base of her skull. She told me afterward, "The hives completely disappeared, as did the stiffness and pain in my neck after one 30-minute session. What a miracle!" She added, "I also feel that I am thinking more clearly and am happier than I have ever been in my life."

I gave Sandy the name of a craniosacral therapist in her hometown, and she has continued to receive CST.

For Steve, receiving CST was also an entirely new experience, but he was very open to it. He'd had long-standing left hip and neck pain, with occasional numbness in his right arm, since fracturing that arm in a motorcycle accident so badly that he'd been in a life-threatening condition from shock and blood loss by the time he arrived at the hospital. I started our session at his pelvis; as his tissue started to soften, he felt tingling down both legs and a cold sensation in his left leg. There was also a very distinctive feeling of his sacrum dropping into my hand. As we worked on his cervical vertebrae, he felt a warmth travel into his right armpit.

Toward the end of the trip, Steve woke up with neck pain; he mentioned to me that the pain gradually lessened throughout the day, which was unusual for him, as once it started it would usually last over a week. My guess is since his sacrum was not as stuck as it had been, his body had a greater capacity to self-correct. Nine months later, Steve e-mailed me, saying: "The issue I had with my hip is almost gone. I have been doing lot of strength work to help build up the muscles around it. The experience I had when I felt my sacrum move when you were doing CST was something I will never forget!"

Another happy update to this story is that he and his wife had been trying to conceive a baby for some time, and not long after he got back home, his wife became pregnant. I had a big smile on my face when I recently received a photo of his beautiful baby daughter.

♡

At the end of the trip, while we were staying in Dubrovnik, I worked on Nancy Levin, the events director for Hay House. Her job requires her to coordinate many activities at once—she is juggling numerous balls in the air during every event! She was kept very busy during our trip, so dialing down her fight-or-flight response was a key aspect of her session. She had never received CST before, but had experienced many other complementary therapies.

The majority of the session was spent opening up structures through her pelvis and releasing her sacrum. As the tissues in this area let go of their tension, a lot of heat was released and she felt tingling down her legs to her feet. Nancy went into a deep state of relaxation as I worked on the fascial tightness around both shoulder blades. I was then able to get some opening in the base of her neck while feeling the vertebrae in her neck change their alignment. I ended by inducing a still point at her occiput.

Nancy lay still for about five minutes as she assimilated what she had experienced. During the trip she had received several insights into personal issues, and having this session at the end of the tour allowed her to integrate what she had learned into her body.

After this session her colleagues asked me what I had done to her, as they had never seen her so chill and relaxed! We all spent the day cruising on a galleon around the Elafiti Islands in the Adriatic Sea, celebrating the end of our time together with dancing. This was the perfect opportunity for Nancy to continue the work we had done together and express the new sense of freedom in her body through dance.

♡

I hope I've provided you with enough ideas here to inspire you in finding your own individual ways to deepen the gains from your sessions. Next, I'll present some simple CST techniques you can perform at home.

Chapter Eight

Craniosacral Therapy at Home

Dr. John Upledger developed craniosacral therapy and taught it outside the osteopathic field because he recognized that almost anybody can learn to perform the techniques effectively and deliver significant therapeutic benefit. For those who don't plan to do the work professionally, he developed a class called ShareCare. It's designed to teach the basics of CST so people come away with some simple and effective hands-on techniques that they can do for their friends and family.

ShareCare has been a fun and exciting class for me to teach. Everybody leaves with a good understanding of the work and feels empowered to do the techniques. They get to know firsthand how we can support and connect to each other in our quest for living with our innate vitality. And they see how simple it is to use these techniques in our everyday lives. While it's always better and easier to learn in person, I'm going to describe a few techniques in this chapter. I believe you'll find that you can use them effectively on yourself, your family, and your friends.

First, though, we'll look at some underlying principles that are important to understand before trying any of the techniques. You'll then learn some common-sense precautions, and you'll also learn about resources that can help you.

Getting Comfortable Working with Energy

All hands-on techniques are bioenergy transfers from one field to another. In CST, the intention is to bring strength and balance to the energy field of the client. I've described how babies and children are particularly aware of the energetic component of CST, being able to sense a hand held off the body and out of sight.

It's quite obvious to me that I'm working with an energetic exchange when I work with animals. For example, I worked on a rabbit that was not able to hop or use his left back leg without tipping to the side. After 15 minutes of CST he could hop on his left leg with minimal tipping. To me, this highlights the energetic component of the work, as I am not at all familiar with the anatomy of a rabbit—and although I followed the soft-tissue changes in my usual way, I was not clear on the structure involved. I relied more than usual on my intuition and, I suspect, responded to unknown energetic subtleties. It's not necessary to be well versed in this energetic aspect, but it is important to have an open mind and to be curious about whatever shows up.

It's natural to wonder where that energy comes from. If we can stay in a place of nonjudgment, we see that it isn't our own energy we're using. If it were, we'd be feeling depleted afterward. Try holding the belief that whatever energy you or your friend needs is available. In other words, hold in your mind that there is an infinite source of energy in whatever form you're looking for. When doing the techniques described in this chapter, it can be helpful to imagine that you're sourcing energy from the earth or the universe.

I've also described sessions in this book where a color of light is brought in; for example, my client may picture a pink light coming into the heart, and I would also imagine the pink light coming in through my hands into their heart. I visualize this light coming in through the top of my head and down through my hands. You can try doing this, too.

There are times when my clients feel that energy needs to be released out of their bodies. They may choose a particular place as the exit area, such as the sacrum, and I would join with them, picturing the energy leaving there. I may imagine it going down into the earth, and often I'll become aware of a pulsing sensation in my feet. There are no hard-and-fast rules about how to bring energy in and let it out of the body. The one idea to stay away from is that it's your job to "do" the work. Be clear in your mind that you're not putting your energy into your friends' bodies, nor taking energy out of them and into your own body.

There are in-depth studies that measured high-frequency energies that come from the surface of the body, and energetic responses to different therapies. If you're interested in reading more on this subject there are many excellent books, including *Infinite Mind* by Valerie Hunt.

Setting Intention and Being Grounded

The intention we hold in this work and, for that matter, everything in our lives is very powerful and takes some careful monitoring. Oftentimes we aren't aware of what we want or what our private conversation is. As you prepare to put your hands on a friend to try a technique, pay attention to the thoughts running through your head. You may want to quietly sit for a moment and monitor yourself: Is your intention about what you want, or about what your loved one wants? As you pay attention to the thoughts running through your head, see if they are holding any judgment about the person you're about to work with.

Even though I'm very experienced, I can still be amazed by my assumptions. Many times I've suddenly become aware that I was incorrect in what I thought somebody wanted from CST. It's vital to align my intentions with those of my client, and this requires listening carefully to both my client's and my own internal chatter. Remember: You are putting your hands on people to support their inner wisdom in finding a way to alleviate their pain or discomfort. You are not there to "fix" them. That's *their* job!

If you're familiar with prayer, you know how to set an intention. Some of you may have participated in a prayer circle; these can be very supportive and helpful. There have been fascinating studies showing how effective prayer can be with health outcomes.

Intentions can also be simple statements of accountability, like the one set by a recent client who said, "I am clearing the source of my shoulder pain, and I am open to whatever shows up as we work on this." An intention you may want to set for yourself as the person putting your hands on is, "I am here as a witness and loving support to my friend's process, and I am paying attention to what I feel through my hands." In talking about CST, Dr. John set a great intention: "We should all love each other . . . that's how we facilitate transformation. Love has to go with those hands."

A good outcome is defined by the person receiving CST—not the practitioner! Taking an honest look at what intentions we may be holding for the person we're working on, we can start to get a clearer sense of what we're doing with our energy. This leads to the questions: *Am I grounded? What happens when I am ungrounded? Am I neutral?*

It's from being grounded and being as neutral as you can that you'll be able to monitor the quality of your touch and maintain the intention you set.

Becoming Grounded

"Being grounded" is a phrase that is commonly used, but many times not well understood. I understand it by how I feel in my body. If I'm aware of how it's feeling right this second, and I'm present to whatever is going on in and around me, I am grounded. It's predominately through my meditation practices that I have come to have a better sense of what being grounded means. Before I knew how to ground myself, I had a sense of wanting to run away from any feelings that made me uncomfortable.

There's a sense of ease and of "being right here" in your body when you're grounded, even in intense situations. In an ungrounded state, you'll feel discomfort or a sense of absence. Many people walk around somewhat ungrounded, and they function fine. But to be present with someone therapeutically, it's essential to be grounded so we can provide a safe, stable presence for the person we're working with. And when we're the client, being grounded is what helps us feel into our bodies.

To better understand the concept of grounding, let's look at the extreme of being ungrounded. I'm sure you can think of situations where your body was cringing with discomfort and embarrassment. Our language has phrases to describe this feeling, like "It made my toes curl up," "I wanted to crawl out of my skin," or "I just wanted to run away." These are all descriptions of what we do when we are no longer grounded or present. Our bodies become tense and can have a paralyzed or frozen quality. Or we may not feel our bodies at all, as if we have left them altogether and are floating around somewhere outside ourselves.

A quick way to ground yourself is to become aware of your feet on the floor and take a scan through your body to see how you're feeling. I do this when I'm first putting my hands on a client, just before assessing. Some therapists have rituals or habits to help remind them to stay present. I like to have both feet planted on the floor, and often take off my shoes so that I have more sensation in my feet. My yoga practice has really helped me with feeling my feet where they contact the ground, noting how my weight is distributed from side to side and front to back, and noticing any sensation such as tingling or pulsing on my soles. This awareness keeps me grounded and in my body.

There are guided meditation practices that help you scan through your body and come into a deeper awareness of what's happening internally for you. My preference is that a body scan be performed from the feet upward, but by all means play with different ways of feeling grounded and get as much guidance as you wish so you can discover your own preference. I found the work of Suzanne Scurlock-Durana, which I mentioned earlier, to be tremendously helpful in developing this ability.

As a session progresses, you'll want to check in with yourself often, asking, *Am I grounded?* If not, you'll use the tools you've developed to reconnect with a sense of ease in your body before you continue.

♡

If you learned to be ungrounded when you were young, it can become a habit and even feel "normal." In this case, you may not know what it's like to be grounded, and must learn how to connect back with your body. Receiving CST is a good way to do that—an experienced therapist can help you identify and feel when you are no longer connected with your body, either altogether or in a specific area. Learn how to be comfortable and grounded in your own body before attempting to perform CST on someone else.

As the therapist, one potential pitfall of being ungrounded is experiencing your clients' symptoms. This happened for me in my early days of practicing CST. After my first class I was working on a friend who had taken a bit of persuasion to be my guinea pig. As I began the ten-step protocol, she started to develop a bad headache. She had sustained a nasty concussion after falling down some stairs a decade previously, and she became worried that this headache would progress like those she'd experienced after her accident. I started to panic—I desperately wanted her pain to go away, not get worse! I just wanted her to have a great CST experience, but this was a recipe for disaster: my intention of being open to her process was lost, I wasn't grounded, and I wasn't neutral. I started to feel drained, and guess what . . . I got a nasty headache, too. All in all, it was very messy.

When something like this happens, the client can leave feeling great and symptom-free, while the therapist is a wreck. But in a case like this, relief for the client will never be long-lasting, as real change hasn't occurred. For example, I worked on a new craniosacral therapist who easily took on her clients' symptoms. She had gotten to the point where she was vomiting after sessions. It didn't take long to restore her equilibrium, but as you can imagine, this is something you want to avoid.

Here's a question to ask yourself to find out if you're susceptible: When you're listening to a friend who's going through something difficult, do you end up feeling tired and generally lousy? If you do, you want to take a look at how practicing being grounded and neutral will help you.

I know that this phenomenon is something that many of us are aware of, as I frequently get asked if I'm exhausted at the end of my day, and clients will sometimes apologize for expressing their deepest emotions, no doubt worried that their emotions will negatively affect me in some way. When we are grounded and neutral, we don't get exhausted performing CST, and we don't take on our clients' symptoms or emotions.

Finding Neutral

The following is a fun and simple exercise for exploring and feeling into the concept of being neutral.

Sit opposite a friend with your knees close to each other, and put your hands on his or her knees. As you place your hands, hold the intention of sending energy through your hands and into his or her body. Pay attention to what it feels like for you to be putting energy in, and have your friend pay attention to his or her own feelings, too. You only need to do this for a few minutes, then gently remove your hands from your friend.

Take a moment for each of you to share your observations. What did this feel like for you? For your friend? Was it comfortable? Intense? Warm? Use all of your senses to describe what you felt.

Now, with the intention of taking energy out, place your hands back on your friend. Stay with that intention for a few minutes, then take some time for observation and feedback once you take your hands off.

Finally, place your hands back on your friend's knees, but this time hold the intention of being neutral, neither putting energy in nor taking it out. While you're doing this, check in to see if it feels neutral to him or her as well. Stay here and play with the sensations to get the feeling of neutral finely tuned. Once you reliably have the feeling of neutral in your hands, change your intention so your hands are providing exactly what your friend needs at this moment.

Get feedback from your friend, and check in with yourself to be sure you're not just falling into a pattern of giving or taking but responding appropriately to what the tissues are asking for. Stay grounded and present.

You will be amazed by how much you learn from this simple exercise. Even though I've done it many, many times, I still like to do it. We can always become more neutral!

Before placing your hands on somebody and carrying out CST techniques, it is important to know whether your tendency is to send energy in or to take it out. It can also be useful information to have in any situation involving touching or holding, particularly when holding a baby and being around children.

Children have a very finely tuned ability to know when a person is grounded. The more grounded and neutral we are, the calmer the child. I clearly observed this once when I was with two other mothers of twins one morning, which meant six ten-month old babies all in my friend's family room! There was a loud bang in the house that alarmed all the little ones, along with the mother whose house we were in. Since their mom was upset, her two children immediately crawled over to me and sat in my lap. They wanted to calm themselves, and sitting with me helped them do that.

I noticed that whenever my own two children are feeling uncertain they like to rest one hand on my knee. Connecting with me physically helps them regulate their own nervous systems. I've practiced being grounded and neutral for many years, so by now it's second nature to me. And it's also very apparent to me when I lose my connection to myself, as it gets reflected back to me by the behavior of my children! Too often I'm in a great hurry to get out of the house and into the car for school and work in the morning. My children will immediately sense this and start whining and losing their focus. It can quickly spiral out of control unless I take a deep breath and reground myself to keep them on track with the shoe-putting-on process and so on to get out of the house.

Another aspect of CST that Dr. John emphasized, one that's also a foundational aspect to the Inquiry Process training I did with Amaran Tarnoff, is being nonjudgmental. Nonjudgment is a necessary quality of neutrality; it's also related to intention, in that it involves striving not to be attached to any particular outcome or behavior, nor counting on loved ones to take any of our suggestions or advice.

How to Feel the Rhythm

Now that you're more informed about what to be aware of energetically when putting your hands on somebody, you're ready to experiment with feeling the craniosacral rhythm (CSR). Remember that the CSR is in two phases: flexion, where there is a rolling out felt in your hands at all the paired bones; and extension, where there is a rolling in felt in your hands at those bones. (If you want to refresh your memory on how the CSR is created, I go into more detail about it in Chapters One and Two.)

♡

Have a friend lie down face up, and start at his or her feet, placing your hands on the tops of the ankles or resting the heels in your hands. Make sure that you have positioned yourself so you can be relaxed and drop your shoulders. It doesn't matter whether you're sitting or standing.

Now that your hands are touching your friend's feet, hold an intention that the CSR come into your hands. Keep your hands light, soft, and relaxed; take the work out of it. The pressure through your hands is, at most, about the weight of a nickel, or five grams. You may want to place a nickel in your hand to appreciate just how light that touch is; see how different that nickel feels when your hand is held light and loose, and when it's held tightly. Memorize the feeling of light and loose.

You may feel only a portion of the CSR to begin with, or sporadically become aware of motion under your hands. If you feel any of this, you are feeling the CSR. Now take your hands off, and check in with your body. It's very likely that you have tensed up somewhere, so let that go, ground yourself, and again place your hands back on your friend's feet. This time, pay attention more to the direction of the motion you feel in your hands: is it extension or flexion? Can you track a complete cycle of the CSR as it rolls all the way out, pauses, then rolls all the way in?

Take another break, and get loose and grounded. Then place your hands on your friend's thighs, and start assessing the CSR again. Take note of what you feel.

Continue in this manner, moving up the body, placing your hands on the paired bones: the sides of the pelvis, the rib cage, the shoulders, and at either side of the head. The ribs can be a challenge, as you may get distracted by the motion of breathing. You might also notice one of the many other rhythms in the body. Since at this moment your intention is to feel the CSR, push the other rhythms out of your awareness. Focus on feeling only the CSR.

As you practice and play with feeling the CSR in these areas, you can start to compare the motion of the CSR in your friend's left and right sides, noting any asymmetries you feel. If you feel a restriction or asymmetry, you can ask him or her if that area is significant: maybe it's painful or it was injured in the past.

It's a great idea to practice on as many different people as possible, as every body feels slightly different.

Still Point

Once you can feel the CSR, you're ready to try a still point. A still point is achieved when you intentionally bring the CSR to a stop as it pauses at the end of an extension. Still points are relaxing for a client because they calm the nervous system, giving the body an opportunity to work on correcting itself. It's an extremely safe technique for anyone who can safely move from lying down to sitting up; you should not perform a still point on people who are too ill or too frail to make that simple movement on their own.

With your friend lying face up, place your hands on the tops of the ankles or under the heels to feel the CSR, and follow a few cycles of the rhythm. Then follow the CSR all the way into extension and allow your hands to become a barrier to motion as the CSR starts to roll out into flexion. This is a subtle action, performed with very little pressure. You are not pushing or rolling in with your hands; you are simply not allowing the structures under your hands to roll outward. You can picture yourself as a wall or a mountain, still and unmovable. You may feel a wobbling motion under your hands as the still point happens; you may feel the tissue under your hands roll further inward.

Once the body is no longer trying to roll out into flexion, stop being a barrier. You can keep your hands on through the duration of the still point, which lasts anywhere from a few seconds to a few minutes, or you can take your hands off. The CSR will start back up spontaneously; you do not need to help it. You may notice that your friend spontaneously takes in a big breath right before you feel the rhythm start again.

It's interesting to keep your hands on during a still point, because even though the CSR is off you may notice other motion, heat, or other signs of tissue response underneath your hands. When the CSR comes back on again, pay attention to how it feels.

Many times you'll notice that it has a greater amplitude and sense of vibrancy. Any asymmetry that was there when you started may have corrected itself. Still points can be induced anywhere on the body—try performing a still point at each of the places on your friend's body where you have practiced feeling the CSR.

A particularly potent place to carry out a still point is on the back of the head, on the occiput. This technique is safe for most everyone but the very sick, with the added caution that it should not be performed on children younger than ten, as their occiputs may not yet be fused into one bone. (If you don't have the expertise to know if your child's occiput is fused, don't perform a still point here!)

To perform the technique, place your two hands, palms up, under the back of the head, with your little fingers touching each other. Your thumbs will be floating off to the side, not involved. Feel the CSR in your fingers and palms. As you feel the motion of extension, follow it all the way in and then create a gentle, easy barrier, just as I described above. Pay more attention to the sensation on the inner halves of your hands, from the little fingers out toward the length of your middle fingers and into your palms. Once you feel that the CSR has stopped trying to roll out into flexion, relax your hands completely and monitor what you feel until it starts again.

You can also induce a still point at the occiput by using a still-point inducer. This device is made out of dense foam with two bumps on it, and you rest the back of your head in between those bumps. As you lie there, your body will go into a still point and will come out of it when it is ready. You don't need to worry about staying there too long, as your body will regulate itself. I usually spend about ten minutes on my still-point inducer to help me unwind from busy days. I can feel tension easing and will often experience jerky movements similar to those I get as I'm falling asleep. This lets me know that my nervous system is resetting itself and finding a better balance point. One of my favorite positions is with my legs up the wall in the yoga pose *viparita karani,* with the still-point inducer placed under my occiput.

You don't have to use a specially made still-point inducer; you can use two tennis balls placed inside a sock, with a knot tied in the middle so that there is about a half-inch gap between the balls. It works just as well, but be aware that dogs will think that it's a toy made for them and not a therapeutic tool for you!

You can also perform a still point on yourself. One of my favorite ways to do this is to place my hands on my thighs while I'm sitting, and then follow my CSR for a few cycles before creating a barrier and inducing a still point.

I once used this to great effect about seven years ago, when I was flying to the UK by myself. We were midway through our flight, so we were over a vast expanse of ice and tundra, when there was a strong smell of burning rubber in the cabin. Nobody was talking about this smell, and I could feel my legs go to jelly with fear. My heart was beating rapidly and my mind was going crazy imagining all sorts of awful scenarios, so I decided to do a still point at my thighs.

Just the act of distracting my mind and having it pay attention to my CSR was helpful. Once I created a still point I could feel my body relax, and my mind stopped racing through possible catastrophic stories. My heart rate dropped, and I spontaneously took in a deep breath. Not long after I felt my adrenaline response settle, there was an announcement made by one of the flight attendants explaining what had happened and reassuring us that it was all under control. I know that if I had not done the still point I would have been jangled and a lot more tired than usual getting off that flight.

Direction of Energy

Another simple technique you can try on your friends (as well as yourself) is called "direction of energy." To do this technique, first make sure that you are grounded and neutral and in a comfortable position. Then place your hands on either side of where there is pain in your friend's body; let's use a shoulder as an example.

Once your hands are on either side of your friend's shoulder, let your hands soften and blend with the skin and tissue of the shoulder. Then imagine that your hands are listening to the shoulder, and you are asking what would help it the most. You may send energy from one hand through to the other, or you may bring energy out. Remember to stay grounded in your body, and present with what's happening. You're there as a support to your friend's inner wisdom.

As your hands blend with the shoulder, pay attention to any changes you feel: maybe there's a sense of warmth, some movement, or pulsing. If you feel movement, you can follow it with your hands. Check in with your friend and ask how the process is feeling—what does he or she notice? Keep your hands in place as long as you feel you need to. I usually ask myself: *Does it feel like I can take my hands off yet?* Once you feel like it's time, slowly disengage from the tissue and lift your hands off the body.

I use this technique when my children have fallen and hurt themselves, when they have a pain somewhere, and when they're sick. I ask them, "Would you like some craniosacral therapy?" When they're really hurt the answer is always yes; in fact they'll often come and ask for it. Children can also do this technique for each other. There is a wonderful children's book called *I Can Show You I Care: Compassionate Touch for Children* by Susan Cotta that describes how they can help each other with a healing touch and positive intention when they are hurt.

Remember that you can also use this technique on yourself; I use this technique frequently for my everyday aches and pains. You don't need to always put both hands on the place that's giving you discomfort. For example, when I had a sinus infection, I placed my thumb and index finger on the bridge of my nose. Then I engaged with my tissue and sent in energy. I could feel the pressure start to lessen and heard a few popping sounds as my airways opened up!

I also relieve shoulder pain by cupping one hand over the upper trapezius muscle that often holds tension for me and placing my other hand over the space between my neck and shoulder on the opposite side. I notice where my attention gets drawn, perhaps underneath my index finger or the palm of my hand. I also notice any changes in my breath and allow spontaneous movements to happen in other parts of my body. I always notice a greater sense of calmness and well-being, and a feeling like my hand is still there for a while afterward.

Jaw Decompression

Another very useful technique to try on yourself will help you let go of tension in the muscles around the jaw. I think that all of us at one time or another have noticed our jaws get tight. It's an automatic response to danger: we clench our teeth and brace for the emergency!

If you know that you clench and grind your teeth at night this is good to do right before you go to sleep and when you wake up in the morning. As you repeat this technique, you'll start to become more aware of tension creeping back in during the day and know how to let it go. This creates a positive feedback loop, providing you with a way to break the cycle of clenching.

Bring the pads of your fingers up to the sides of your lower jaw and find the place where the teeth meet the bone. There is a perfect little ledge there to rest the pads of your fingertips—let your fingers rest at that ledge and relax your arms. Then, mainly with intention, imagine that you are bringing your jaw down toward your feet. Do not physically pull with your fingers: the muscles around the jaw are very sensitive and know when you're telling them what to do; they will resist! Just let the weight of your relaxed, steady hands bring your jaw downward.

Become curious about what you feel, take your time, and pay attention to the sensation of letting go. You will know when you have completed the technique, as your hands will naturally lift off.

♡

I hope that you're feeling inspired and empowered to carry out some of these simple yet effective hands-on techniques at home. Be sure to bring out the playful side of yourself as you try them! Being too serious about this only increases tension in your body, and that doesn't help anyone.

AFTERWORD

My wish is that you found this to be a useful book, and that you're excited to experience the benefits of craniosacral therapy. May it help guide you and your loved ones on your journeys toward greater health and well-being.

As we come to a close, I'd like to share with you a little more about the time I worked with Lina, the six-year-old with rheumatoid arthritis whom I mentioned in Chapter Six. When I'd worked in intensive care units as a physical therapist at the beginning of my career, I had not felt comfortable or accepted, and questioned my role there. This time, walking in as a craniosacral therapist to help care for Lina, I knew deep in my heart what my role was. I was also welcomed and accepted by all the staff. We could see her vital signs improving while I worked, which was the ultimate proof to me that CST can truly complement and support a person's healing in any environment.

The icing on the cake was being able to empower Denise, Lina's mom, as I performed a few CST techniques on her and taught her how to be grounded and induce a still point on her daughter. Denise and I got the feeling of coming full circle together: she is an emergency-room nurse learning firsthand how to incorporate CST into her life, and I've been incorporating the CST skills I've learned over the last ten years into the most mainstream areas of conventional medicine. Not only did we share on this professional level, we also connected our hands and hearts and were able to channel our strong mother energy into helping young Lina through a life-threatening event.

I'd like to end this book with a quote from Dr. John that continues to inspire me:

> The secret something that is shared in effective healing methods is the process of leading the patient to an honest and truthful self-discovery. This self-discovery is required for the initiation and continuation of self-healing; for it is only through

> self-healing—in contrast to curing—that patients can experience both permanent recovery and spiritual growth. When there is a very close correspondence between self-image and truth, our self-healing powers may be virtually unlimited.

From all of my studies and experience, I've come to believe that there's an intelligence, a consciousness, in every cell of our bodies, and that there's also a mystery beyond my knowing. In a recent CST session I received, I got to experience and picture just how vast and infinite our energetic selves are. I felt and saw in my body that we are capable of moving our attention between microscopic cells in our bodies to the expanse of the universe, creating infinite possibilities for health and healing. It is this awareness that keeps CST exciting and alive for me, and my hope is it will for you, too.

Please share what you learn with your friends and loved ones. I send love from my hands and heart to yours.

GLOSSARY

arcing: a technique used to identify where energy cysts are being held in the body.

avenue of expression: a phrase used in the Upledger teachings that incorporates all the structures in and around the mouth and throat that are involved in speech.

blending and melding: a method of touching a person with the least amount of intrusion possible, during which a therapist allows, trusts, and accepts the information that comes into his or her hands.

cellular memory: the theory that cells have their own experience of life and can remember events that affect them.

central nervous system (CNS): the brain and spinal cord.

cerebrospinal fluid (CSF): the fluid that bathes the brain and spinal cord, providing nourishment and cushion, and removing waste.

comprehensive therapy program: a program run by the Upledger Institute in which a person can receive multihands CST and other forms of treatment over a five-day period in a group setting.

Continuum Movement: a method that explores how bodies move when there are no demands placed on them, in which you use breath and sounds to vibrate through tissue and loosen restrictions.

craniosacral rhythm (CSR): the rhythmic movement created by the slight change in volume of the cerebrospinal fluid that flows through the craniosacral system.

craniosacral system: made up of the central nervous system, the cerebrospinal fluid and the membranes that contain it, and the bones that attach to those membranes.

cranium: another name for the skull.

dura mater: the outer membrane of the meninges, which creates the watertight container for the cerebrospinal fluid.

emotional holding: a reference to the theory that the body holds emotions and tension from significant life events when we cannot fully feel and experience at the time that those events occur. We put them "on hold," to be dealt with later.

energy cyst: the result of the body's compressing foreign, disorganized energy into a contained space. The trauma that introduced this disorganized energy may be physical, chemical, or emotional.

extension: when used in relation to the craniosacral rhythm, this term describes the rolling-in phase (internal rotation) of the CSR.

fascia: fibrous, protein-packed tissue with varying degrees of flexibility that provides internal structure and support for the body.

flexion: when used in relation to the craniosacral rhythm, this term describes the rolling-out phase (external rotation) of the CSR.

grounded: a state of feeling present in our bodies and connected to our surroundings; a sense of ease and of "being right here" in your body.

hyoid: a horseshoe-shaped bone located at the throat.

inner wisdom: also referred to as the "inner physician," a term coined by Dr. John Upledger. It describes the part of ourselves that knows what we need to heal. The client's inner wisdom is the guide to any CST treatment and can be communicated with out loud through dialogue or through monitoring changes in the CSR in response to questions.

Inquiry Process: a particular kind of conversation, developed by Amaran Tarnoff, composed of asking and answering questions that support people in discovering what their barriers are to producing results, and what they need to do or learn to get through those barriers.

meninges: the three membranes (the dura, pia and arachnoid) that envelop the brain and spinal cord.

mouth work: any craniosacral technique carried out inside the mouth.

multihands: the term for having two or more craniosacral therapists working on a client at the same time.

neutral: a nonjudgmental therapeutic presence.

occiput: the bone at the back of the head.

palpation: touch for the therapeutic purpose of determining the condition of specific structures in the body and energy field.

rock and glide: a CST technique in which one hand is placed under the cranium and the other under the sacrum, using the CSR to help mobilize the dural tube and free any restrictions.

sacrum: the triangle-shaped bone at the base of the spine.

significance detector: a complete stop in the CSR, occurring spontaneously, which indicates that there is a therapeutic change in the client's body.

SomatoEmotional Release (SER): a phenomenon that occurs when, as the local tissue under a therapist's hand is responding and changing, there is a simultaneous ripple effect of response and change in other areas of the body. Emotions may or may not be experienced by the client at this time.

sphenoid: butterfly-shaped bone that forms part of the cranium; the outer wings can be felt at the temples.

still point: intentionally stopping the CSR. Therapists may induce a still point by following the flexion and extension of the rhythm, and then using their hands to very gently create a stop at the end of an extension. This allows an opportunity for the body to self-correct and clear areas that are restricted or not running smoothly.

sutures: the joint or connections between the bones that make up the cranium.

ten-step protocol: a protocol of techniques taught at the Upledger Institute that creates a safe and gentle way to treat the whole body.

unwinding: supporting a limb in which a restriction or energy cyst has been identified and allowing for a spontaneous release of tissue to happen through nondirected movement.

RESOURCES

My website is: **www.HealingBodyBalance.com**
My mailing address is: P.O. Box 3502, Livermore, CA 94550

Craniosacral Therapy

www.upledger.com

This website contains information on classes, how to find a practitioner, and comprehensive therapy programs, including work with dolphins. You can purchase still-point inducers and the many books that Dr. John wrote. You may also contact them at:

Upledger Institute International, Inc.
11211 Prosperity Farms Rd., Suite D-325
Palm Beach Gardens, FL 33410
561-622-4334
800-233-5880 (toll-free)
561-622-4771 (fax)

www.ultimate-yu.com

Here you can find out more information about CST with dolphins by Barbara Huntress Tresness. Her DVD *Celebration of Healing* can be purchased by contacting her at barb@ultimate-yu.com or 315-569-0584.

www.aboutfacehealing.com

This website offers information about CST tailored specifically for veterans.

www.becalm.ca

You can order Becalm Balls here, which are a different type of still-point inducer.

Continuum Movement

www.continuummovement.com

This website provides information on classes, finding Continuum teachers in your area, and suggested DVDs and books.

Halliwick Swimming

www.halliwick.org.uk

The website of the Halliwick Association of Swimming Therapy in the UK offers more information on how the Halliwick concept supports people, especially those with disabilities, experience freedom in the water. Their book, *Halliwick Swimming for Disabled People,* is a good practical guide to their work.

Yoga

www.specialyoga.org

This is the website of the program Yoga for the Special Child. Get information on teaching yoga to children with special needs, find a teacher of this program in your area, and purchase the book *Yoga for the Special Child* by Sonia Sumar.

www.bksiyengar.com

This is the official website of Iyengar yoga. I recommend the book *Yoga: The Path to Holistic Health* by BKS Iyengar, which provides detailed information and photographs of poses.

Yoga: Awakening the Inner Body by Donald Moyer. This book is for people who already have yoga experience. It is good for precise detail and for working on specific areas of the body.

Yoga for Computer Users and *Yoga for Healthy Knees* by Sandy Blaine. These books offer basic poses to help with specific issues in the body. They give good instruction along with photographs.

Moving Toward Balance by Rodney Yee. This is a helpful guide if you would like to start a regular home practice. It explains sequences of poses with photographs.

Stories and Poetry

www.nancylevin.com

Nancy Levin's *Writing for My Life . . .* is a beautiful book of poetry inspired by a time in her life that was full of major transitions. Nancy's poems convey what is difficult to put into words when describing healing and transformation, just as her poem "whole" did at the beginning of this book.

www.clarissapinkolaestes.com

Clarissa Pinkola Estés is an acclaimed author, poet, and pscyhoanalyst. Her website gives you a full list of her works. My highlights are her audiobook *The Dangerous Old Woman* and the book (also offered as an audiobook) *Women Who Run With the Wolves.*

Information on Energy

www.brucelipton.com

The website of Bruce Lipton, cell biologist by training and an internationally recognized leader in new biology. His work, like CST, combines current scientific discoveries with what is happening on the energetic level. You'll find a list of his books, CDs, and DVDs. I recommend *The Biology of Belief,* which provides in-depth information on the functioning of cells in a very readable format.

www.valerievhunt.com

The website of research scientist Valerie Hunt, a pioneer in the field of bioenergy. Here you'll find a list of her research and publications. I recommend her book *Infinite Mind* for detailed information on her research on the human bioenergy field.

www.lynnemctaggart.com

Lynne McTaggart is a researcher in the fields of medicine and quantum physics, providing a bridge between science and spirituality. If you would like to delve deeper into the research on how energy healing works, her book *The Field* is a great read.

Other Experts Whose Work I Recommend

Wayne Dyer is an internationally renowned author and speaker in the field of self-development. For information on upcoming events, books, CDs, and DVDs, visit: **www.waynedyer.com** or **www.hayhouse.com**.

Suzanne Scurlock-Durana is a noted craniosacral therapist whose work I mentioned in this book. For information on her CDs, workshops, and her book *Full Body Presence*, please visit: **www.healingfromthecore.com**.

Peter Levine is an expert on somatic experiencing (SE). For information on classes, to find practitioners in SE, and for books written by Peter Levine, please visit: **www.traumahealing.com**.

Cheryl Richardson has dedicated her life to teaching the importance of self-care. Her book *The Art of Extreme Self Care* gives clear steps in taking care of yourself that support the ideas I described in Chapter Seven of this book. Please visit her website to find out where she is speaking and see all her publications: **www.cherylrichardson.com**.

ACKNOWLEDGMENTS

I would like to acknowledge the two people who have influenced me the most in the creation of this book: Dr. John Upledger and Dr. Wayne Dyer.

In March 2012 I was attending a celebration of more than 30 years of craniosacral therapy at the Upledger Institute, at a conference called Beyond the Dura. There were several presentations about the developer of CST, Dr. John Upledger, and the legacy of his work. He was a visionary in the field of health care, having dedicated his life to synthesizing complex medical information and putting it into an understandable, usable format. He passionately believed that CST should be accessible to everybody, and that we all have the ability to carry out the work. As I sat surrounded by hundreds of talented therapists, all focused on empowering our clients to heal from within, I felt so lucky to have been trained in the work Dr. John developed, and to be a part of this generation of therapists who are taking his work forward.

While at the conference I learned that Dr. Wayne Dyer was staying with his family only a short distance away, and I ended up carrying out a couple of CST sessions with him. It was during those sessions that I recognized the similarities between two of my most influential teachers. Like Dr. John, Wayne had a hardscrabble upbringing in Detroit, Michigan. And he too is a visionary thinker in the field of self-empowerment and spirituality. As Dr. John did, Wayne has taken complex information and synthesized it into a readable, accessible format. Both have shown dedication to empowering people to make the types of changes in their lives they desire, and they want everyone to benefit from their work.

Wayne, I feel immense gratitude to have such a wonderful friendship and connection with you and your family. My life has changed in so many rich and wonderful ways from knowing you. "Thank you" is not enough, but I keep saying it anyway!

Another teacher who had immense influence on me is Amaran Tarnoff—thank you for creating such powerful, life-changing teachings.

I am indebted to Mata Amritanandamayi (Amma), who is the most inspirational person I have ever met; she has influenced everything in my life.

Thank you to the Upledger Institute for always supporting me, every therapist who has trained with you, and the craniosacral therapy field as a whole. A special thank you to my teachers Tim Hutton and Suzanne Scurlock-Durana, who taught me what excellent craniosacral therapists look, sound, and act like. They, along with Carol McLellan, also gave of their time and provided me with valuable feedback for this book.

I have deep gratitude for my friend and CST colleague Robyn Scherr, who was divinely placed in my life to support the editing process along with coaching and coaxing my writing skills. This book would not have been written without you, my friend!

Thank you to Michael and Jolie Goorjian and Maya for taking the time to read my manuscript and provide me with valuable insight in a gentle and loving way, from the perspective of a receiver rather a doer of the work. And to Lauren for her meticulous proofreading—you are angel sent.

Without Hay House this book would not exist. You are all so special and inspirational to me, and from knowing you all so many doors have opened up for me. A special thank-you to Louise, Reid, Nancy, Stacey, Shannon, and Christy.

A big thanks to my mother, Wendy; my parents-in-law Jim and Celia; and my sisters Jane and Sara, who along with their families have sent encouragement from across the pond.

A heartfelt thanks to my fairy godmother Kate and her husband, Jim, who—along with my friends Jen, Cat, and Kat—have supported me and my family through the process of writing this book in every practical way possible. Along with the staff of Valley Montessori School, who provide an environment for my children to thrive, giving me the peace of mind I have needed to write *From My Hands and Heart.*

I am grateful to my friends Kate and Jim Coughlin for creating the sacred space of Downtown Yoga that has been my sanctuary—*Namaste.*

Thank you to all my friends who show up at just the right time and offer their friendship and talents: Paola, Amanda, Fariba, Kate M, Diane, Lori, Donna, Pip, Jessica, Neal, Debra, Greg, Jennifer, Heather, Amy, and Katja.

Thank you for all the support and cheerleading from my clients who provided the motivation for me to write, and to the many who took the time to write about their experiences for this book.

My multihands group and CST sisters Kathy Lorenz, Sarah Woodard, Iris Ratowsky, Trisha Parish, Cheeta Llanes, and Robyn Scherr have been my rock—thank you.

Thank you to all my swim coaches: Diane, Adrianna, Alex, and Genii; and my swimming buddies—you have kept me sane!

And last but most definitely not least, to my husband, Andy! He has never failed to support me as I have followed my dreams, this book being one of them. Just like some CST experiences, words don't express the feeling. The depth of love and gratitude I feel are beyond words.

ABOUT THE AUTHOR

Kate Mackinnon has been working as a physical therapist for more than 20 years, supporting people in creating comfort and ease in their bodies. She finds that craniosacral therapy is the key to effecting speedy, long-lasting recoveries in her patients, while also increasing the effectiveness of any other treatments they receive. She lives, works, and swims in Livermore, California.

For more information, please visit:
www.healingbodybalance.com.

NOTES

NOTES

NOTES

NOTES

NOTES

NOTES

NOTES

NOTES

NOTES

NOTES

NOTES

NOTES

NOTES

We hope you enjoyed this Hay House book. If you'd like to receive our online catalog featuring additional information on Hay House books and products, or if you'd like to find out more about the
Hay Foundation, please contact:

Hay House, Inc., P.O. Box 5100, Carlsbad, CA 92018-5100
(760) 431-7695 or (800) 654-5126
(760) 431-6948 (fax) or (800) 650-5115 (fax)
www.hayhouse.com® • www.hayfoundation.org

♡

Published and distributed in Australia by: Hay House Australia Pty. Ltd., 18/36 Ralph St., Alexandria NSW 2015 • *Phone:* 612-9669-4299
Fax: 612-9669-4144 • www.hayhouse.com.au

Published and distributed in the United Kingdom by: Hay House UK, Ltd., Astley House, 33 Notting Hill Gate, London W11 3JQ • *Phone:* 44-20-3675-2450
Fax: 44-20-3675-2451 • www.hayhouse.co.uk

Published and distributed in the Republic of South Africa by:
Hay House SA (Pty), Ltd., P.O. Box 990, Witkoppen 2068
Phone/Fax: 27-11-467-8904 • www.hayhouse.co.za

Published in India by: Hay House Publishers India, Muskaan Complex, Plot No. 3, B-2, Vasant Kunj, New Delhi 110 070 • *Phone:* 91-11-4176-1620
Fax: 91-11-4176-1630 • www.hayhouse.co.in

Distributed in Canada by: Raincoast,
9050 Shaughnessy St., Vancouver, B.C. V6P 6E5 •
Phone: (604) 323-7100 • *Fax:* (604) 323-2600 • www.raincoast.com

Take Your Soul on a Vacation

Visit **www.HealYourLife.com®** to regroup,
recharge, and reconnect with your own magnificence.
Featuring blogs, mind-body-spirit news, and
life-changing wisdom from Louise Hay and friends.

Visit **www.HealYourLife.com** today!

Free e-newsletters from Hay House, the Ultimate Resource for Inspiration

Be the first to know about Hay House's dollar deals, free downloads, special offers, affirmation cards, giveaways, contests, and more!

Get exclusive excerpts from our latest releases and videos from ***Hay House Present Moments***.

Enjoy uplifting personal stories, how-to articles, and healing advice, along with videos and empowering quotes, within ***Heal Your Life***.

Have an inspirational story to tell and a passion for writing? Sharpen your writing skills with insider tips from ***Your Writing Life***.

Sign Up Now!

Get inspired, educate yourself, get a complimentary gift, and share the wisdom!

http://www.hayhouse.com/newsletters.php

Visit www.hayhouse.com to sign up today!

HealYourLife.com

Heal Your Life One Thought at a Time . . . on Louise's All-New Website!

"Life is bringing me everything I need and more."

— Louise Hay

Come to HEALYOURLIFE.COM today and meet the world's best-selling self-help authors; the most popular leading intuitive, health, and success experts; up-and-coming inspirational writers; and new like-minded friends who will share their insights, experiences, personal stories, and wisdom so you can heal your life and the world around you . . . one thought at a time.

Here are just some of the things you'll get at HealYourLife.com:

- DAILY AFFIRMATIONS
- CAPTIVATING VIDEO CLIPS
- EXCLUSIVE BOOK REVIEWS
- AUTHOR BLOGS
- LIVE TWITTER AND FACEBOOK FEEDS
- BEHIND-THE-SCENES SCOOPS
- LIVE STREAMING RADIO
- "MY LIFE" COMMUNITY OF FRIENDS

PLUS:
FREE Monthly Contests and Polls
FREE BONUS gifts, discounts, and newsletters

Make It Your Home Page Today!

www.HealYourLife.com®

HEAL YOUR LIFE®